Stay
fr
Buttercups

The Journey of the
South Downs Triple

Written and performed by
Richard Sterry

First published in Great Britain in 2013

Photographs © Anne Dickins, Mike Anton, Judy McNeill, Steve Golding & Richard Sterry
Cover picture by Anne Dickins

More details about the author can be found at
www.sterry.org
email richard@sterry.org
Twitter @HillBurner

Disclaimer

Whilst every effort has been made to ensure the contents of this book are as accurate as possible, no one mentioned in the book can accept any responsibility for any damage, injury or loss sustained as a result of this material. Professional advice was sought for the training and the endurance mountain biking, it is therefore advisable for anyone wanting to do anything similar to seek professional advice.
Take responsibility for your own actions.
The products and brand names mentioned are based on those used, other brands are also available.

To YOU

I hope this inspires you to turn
your crazy dream
into a reality.

Contents

Richard Sterry is just an ordinary bloke
with a crazy idea and buckets of determination.

Preface

Stranded on the open hill tops in thick fog I had to stay on the grassy track without any assistance from visible landmarks or a GPS. Resorting to nature I could see the buttercups only grew on the edge of the trail. Staying away from the buttercups kept me on the track.

Life is full of mixed messages and it can be confusing on which way to go. Even if we have a clear focus, there are often pretty flowers that lure us away from our goal. Recognising the temptations is one thing, resisting them is another.

If you are a cyclist, the appeal of the South Downs Way in the South of England is one of the Must-Do mountain biker's rides. To complete the full 100 mile length is one thing but to achieve it 3 times in succession is in a league of its own. This book describes the journey of the Triple ride, which dips into several technical areas that may help you achieve your next cycling quest.

For those that have a dream or a crazy goal, this book takes you on the journey how my challenge was conceived, established, planned and conquered. Even when my body was giving up on me for the second time, the deep rooted focus and determination gave me the strength to see it through to the finish.

This book is just not about me setting out to achieve a personal ambition. Along the way many other people joined in with the journey by being part of the support crew, riding with me along the route, following my progress on-line, commenting on the Singletrack World forum, or joining in with the Twitter conversations. It is the contribution by all the onlookers and supporters that has made the journey so memorable and worthwhile. I want to thank everyone for volunteering to play their part and helping me to make a piece of history.

After the ride I was physically and mentally broken. Putting my experience into print has helped me through the recovery process. I also want to share my journey with you to inspire and assist you to achieve more than you think is possible.

Introduction

It felt so wrong; laid out in a car park with my body shivering and wrapped in blankets. Caring words came from those close to me whilst a sense of urgency and concern could be heard in the voices of those directing others. I had to get up but my body wouldn't move. Why wasn't I riding my bike? I had to get to Winchester.

This is a story of an ordinary bloke with a crazy idea, taking him mentally and physically way beyond the point where others, rather sensibly, decide to stop.

The incredible journey ventures into the unknown where very few people have been before. The risks were high so the preparation was meticulous. The journey of a lifetime brought many people together on the South Downs, watched by several hundred on-line.

For many years the South Downs Way has been an aspired challenge in the South East by walkers, runners and cyclists. The 100 mile bridleway stretches from Eastbourne to Winchester, virtually all off road. As it traverses over the tops of the chalk hills, many cyclists have undertaken the route in 2 or 3 days where the more adventurous aim for a single day.

It really doesn't matter how long people take to complete the South Downs Way. The fact that they are giving the beast a go is an achievement. Some people who have not ridden the trail from end to end underestimate the toughness of the route. I have much admiration for anyone attempting to take on the length of the South Downs Way.

The hills are relentless, the gates are endless and the chalk is slippery when wet. To ride the 100 miles between Winchester and Eastbourne is hard, to ride the 200 miles of the South Downs Double is really tough. Only 24 people have completed the Double where many others set out in the hope of getting into the exclusive Hall of Fame. No one had attempted to ride the South Downs Triple.

The second leg of the Double is about twice as hard as the first leg. The third leg of the Triple is about twice as hard as the second leg. The South Downs Triple is a monster of a ride.

Riding a Double in less than 23 hours is tough. To then continue on to ride a further 100 miles sounds just crazy.

The odds were all stacked against me but I was determined to do it. There was only one chance to be the first person to complete the South Downs Triple. It therefore had to be done right. Was I mad? Probably. Was I definitely going to do it? Yes.

During this story of the South Downs Triple there are huge challenges and setbacks that need to be overcome in conditions of extreme tiredness and fatigue. The mental strength and determination required to keep going is immense. My body gave up on me twice during the ride where I had to find the energy to get back on the bike and cycle another 35 and then 60 miles.

The challenge of the South Downs Triple is mental in both senses; it is also an inspiration to anyone who wants to redefine their limits to achieve more than they think currently is possible.

Preparation

Ready?

Thursday 30th May 2012

"You do realise that the best weather window starts tomorrow…"

Tomorrow?!!! We were due to start our 36 hour "journey" on Sunday and it was currently Thursday morning.

"But I'm not ready, how can we possibly reorganise all the logistics and support crew at this short notice?" The date had previously been set and this last minute change was unsettling. I like to be organised and my focus was for starting in 3 day's time.

We had talked about needing to be flexible, but is it possible to bring it forward by 2 days at this late notice?

"Have a think about it and let me know" said the calm voice of friend Simon Usher, who was managing the support. "We can sort out the logistics if you are mentally ready to ride"

Simon is a real down to earth practical guy who is either endurance racing or providing pit crew support for other racers.

He also dropped into the conversation "Oh, and the wind has changed direction." Sowing the seed that another major change may be imminent. All tensed up, I couldn't contemplate two major decisions so I just thought about the change of date.

I paused for a moment. This was going to be the ride of my life, where I only had one chance to do the South Downs Triple. Sitting outside the office canteen basking in the sunshine I munched through a rather large portion of pasta with tuna and bottle green peas. The warm fresh air with the singing birds was a most welcoming sound as I contemplated having to go back to the sterile air conditioned office. It wasn't a difficult decision, I was excited about riding the Triple and I love being on my bike.

A day in the office, or a couple of days on the bike?

Noting all the important things that needed to be done in the next few hours before the ride, I then made my decision.

He was right and I was ready - PANIC!

Everything was a whirr, there was so much to do. What do I do first?

In an awkward phone call I spoke to my boss to scrounge an immediate day and a half off. Working for a large international company my boss had only a functional grasp of the English language. Everything had to be explained in short simple sentences. He was aware of my challenge and fortunately understood the urgency of my request. In a hurried conversation I then explained the situation to my team as I prepared to leave the office. They were not cyclists and couldn't really understand the enormity of the challenge I had set out to do, however they were all very supportive of my insane venture and wished me well.

My mind was in a spin as I ran about pulling everything together. Taking a short break I prepared a list of the essential things to do. It quickly became very long and looked impossible to complete.

"Have you got access to a forecast? The one I am looking at has strong easterlies on Saturday...." Came a text from Simon. Looking on my computer I could see he was right. Do I really want to be riding into a strong head wind on the last section?

My spread sheet preparation and the logistics had been planned based on a WEWE (Winchester-Eastbourne-Winchester-Eastbourne) and now we were going to need to re-plan for EWEW. Fortunately I had saved version 1 of my plans that were originally in the form of EWEW. After some quick reformatting of the spread sheet I ran out a copy with loads of space for the ad hoc notes, there was no time to rejig and type in all my requirements. Emailing this to Simon and Anne, Simon's partner, it left them with the headache of adjusting the logistics again for the support crew to meet the new geographical changes.

My daughter Lorna was really helpful. I had planned to fill a number of envelopes for the support crew to open at intervals along the way and had labelled them with the check point names. The switch of direction meant we had to rename them all and check the contents were appropriate for the location and time of day. 15 large envelopes were sprawled out across the living room floor as we stuffed them with the selection of goodies. The plan was to keep the support crew motivated and nourished so they were at their best to help me when I got tired. Lorna finished off packing and sealing the envelopes before stacking them in order into a large box. Lorna, like me, is into detail and will keep going until the task is finished. She's very focused and good at asking questions, we've had some great chats about anything and everything. It's sometimes difficult as a teenager to be understood and as a parent I try hard to comprehend her outlook on life. Our chats may not solve the world's problems but by keeping the communication channels open hopefully if there is a major issue, Lorna will know that I am there for her.

Simon came over in the early evening to see how I was doing. Stuff was everywhere; food, powdered drink, bike spares, tools, and a pile of clothes to last me a month. A slight look of despair came over his face as he saw the chaos. He too had taken time off work and was about to invest a lot of time to support me with my crazy idea. Looking around he wondered how on earth we could get the show on the road.

"What do you want me to do?" he asked in trying to sense if I had any priorities amongst the confusion.

He helped me to fit the saddle pouches, pumps, GPS and phone each with their own battery packs to the bikes. Normally I carry everything in my back pack but when racing it is all attached to the bike. This enables me to swap over the back packs when the drink runs out. Fortunately I had worked out where everything should go but it's not until you actually put it all together that you realise a cable isn't quite long enough or there is a clash between two bits. Simon was brilliant, he calmly just got on with it while I was still trying to think of the fifteen million things to do and achieving very little.

Eventually the bikes were complete, everything was bundled into boxes and stacked into the Black Pig (Simon's van). There was not much more that I could now do except to try and relax.

Relax, how do I do that? My mind was still spinning and thinking about the pending ride. Had I done enough to prepare?

The pre-event day was scheduled to be one of rest and relaxation with loads of sleep. In reality it was the complete opposite and in some ways this may have helped. I'm not good at doing nothing and would have probably ended up in a bundle of nerves.

The South Downs Way

Situated in the South East of England are the lumpy hills of the South Downs that spread sideways across the country. The vast open spaces on the hill tops provide fantastic views out to sea on one side and on a clear day the North Downs can be seen when looking towards London.

Trails on the South Downs have been around for many centuries as they were drier alternatives to the surrounding wetlands. Later a route over the South Downs was used for safety to transport the valuable goods from the coast to the then capital of England, Winchester.

It wasn't until 1972 that the South Downs Way was recognised. It then stretched 80 miles from Beachy Head to Butser Hill. After the M3 was completed the South Downs Way was extended to Winchester in 1995. The South Downs then became Britain's 15th National Park in 2010. It is the only National trail entirely within a single National Park.

Based on chalk the trails on the South Downs can be fast and flowing when dry in the summer but as soon as it rains they are dangerously slippery. Descending a chalky slope is an art in the wet. The best way is to pick a line and stay on it, if you try to veer left or right you'll hit the deck. The rainwater often creates deep gullies that are treacherous if they catch your wheels.

The terrain of the South Downs Way is either going up or going down, rarely are there flat sections. Depending on who you ask, the amount of climbing for one length of the South Downs Way is between 10,000 and 13,600 feet. My GPS measured around 11,600 feet for each leg, totalling 34,700 feet for the Triple. That is nearly 6 vertical miles, or similar to the cruising height of jet aeroplanes.

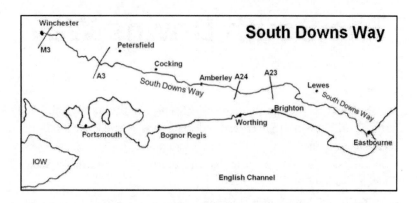

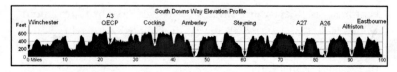

"Hey Garry, have you seen this?" as I showed a page of MBR (Mountain Bike Rider) to my good friend Garry Hall.

"Why don't you do it?" I suggested as he had previously ridden the Trans Wales challenge and was looking for something new.

He looked briefly at the full page Ad for the BHF (British Heart Foundation) 100 mile Randonnée ride on the South Downs.

"I'll give it a go" he replied in his usual brash but casual way.

"Only if you join me?" he continued.

"Er, OK" I said rather hesitantly knowing that it was going to be a very long ride. Previously my longest ride was around 35 miles. This was going to be quite a challenge.

And so it was, back in 2007 Garry and I rode the South Downs Way from Winchester to Eastbourne. It was a monster of a ride where we really struggled on the final hills. We eventually rolled into Eastbourne after 14 hours of riding, with daylight fading, and were completely knackered.

Persuaded to return the following year with another friend, Gareth Ashton, I loved the ride. This time we reached Eastbourne in just 11:20 hours.

Then, for some reason I decided to go for the South Downs Double. All the factors were against me as I had only ever ridden 100 miles twice previously and not ridden much on my own. The all night solo ride would be a new experience and I had only ever been up all night once as a teenager. I had no idea about training or measuring heart rates, I just used to get on the bike and ride. Stretching and nutritional plans were non-existent.

The motivational speaker Steve McDermott suggests when setting SMART goals, (Specific, Measurable, Achievable, Realistic and Timely) not to use the A and R for Achievable and Realistic, but have a goal that is Awesome and Ridiculous.

It was a ridiculous challenge for a person of my limited cycling experience where at the time of planning, only 4 top riders had succeeded with a sub-24 hour time for the 200 mile ride. More importantly, it was also an awesome challenge, which spurred me on to do my homework, seek expert help, commit my soul to it, and take the trophy in 2009 when I succeeded.

The South Downs Way is such a lovely route with its hills and views. It is strangely addictive so I was back again in 2010 riding the BHF Randonnée. Although I managed a sub-10 hour time for the single leg, I still wanted more. The times for the Double were plummeting beyond my reach so I had to find something different.

Whilst on a training ride for 24 Hours of Exposure, my first ever 24 hour solo race, I glided effortlessly along the trails and the hills appeared flat. Feeling as though I could ride forever I wondered why races only go up to 24 hours. Thinking about a longer event, the South Downs Triple was conceived. It was one of those moments of wishful thinking when I felt that anything was possible. Riding three lengths of the South Downs Way back to back in one go, could it be done? The thought buzzed around my head. It ticked the box for being an Awesome and Ridiculous goal, and I like that type of challenge. Could it really be done? Could I do it?

Finishing the 24 Hours of Exposure race in Scotland in 6th place; this was a tougher course than my Double ride on the

South Downs and I was not as exhausted. If my fitness and riding knowledge had improved since the Double, how much more did I need to improve to do the Triple? Perhaps I could do the Triple, but why hadn't anyone done it before? Could I be the first? Now there's a challenge.

I smiled to myself and felt a warm glow inside. What an incredible challenge. This is a goal to top all others and if I was the first, I would be on the podium forever.

Deeply satisfied with a new purpose for riding, I started to work out how I was going to achieve my mission.

Developing the Crazy Idea

I'm a logical person; if I can see that practically something can be done and I want to do it, I'll give it a go. Noting down all the extra considerations for a 36 hour ride compared to a 24 hour event, I reasoned each aspect until I realised that it could be possible. This wasn't a simple exercise, I really had to think through all the difficulties and options to convince myself that riding for 300 miles over two days and one night was realistic. If there was the remotest doubt in my mind that it couldn't be done, now was the time to stop. Beyond this point, failure was not an option.

Having committed myself, I bounced the idea off my cycling friend Anne Dickins. She paused, and then gave a very cautious noncommittal answer. Anne kept looking at me to see if I was joking, but then she saw that I was serious, deadly serious. Normally our rides were quite chatty, but we carried on riding through the woods at Limpsfield Chart without another word being spoken. I could tell the cogs were turning in her head as she tried to comprehend my crazy idea.

A few months later the idea of the Triple was not going away, the more I thought about it, the more I wanted to do it. No one had ever attempted or succeeded in completing the 300 miles on the South Downs. I wanted to be the first. I so desperately wanted to tell people about it, but had to keep it under wraps for fear of someone else going before me. It was hard but I decided not to tell anyone else.

I remember the first time I met Anne; friend Louise Poynton, the Group Sports Editor for the Surrey Mirror, knew us both and suggested that we should get together. Anne had qualified for the 24 hour solo World Championships in Australia and was looking for some help. In July 2010 I nervously sent Anne a text and was surprised to immediately get a reply. My ability to text was slow, we exchanged a few messages and arranged to meet up for a ride.

All my feelings of apprehension before meeting Anne evaporated when she welcomed me into her house. She exuded a warm personality making her very easy to talk to. We chatted over a mug of tea when Ant Jordan, her riding partner arrived, then we prepared to set off for a jaunt.

Within metres of leaving her house, we were weaving our way through the twisty single track in the woods. This theme dominated the ride as we sped between the trees interspersed by a few bomb holes and steep drops. There were one or two drops that I would not have ridden if I'd seen them before I was half way down. Trusting in Anne's line, I just went for it. She was a bit surprised that I followed her.

As the sun set on the beautiful summer's evening, the mysteries of the woods lay beneath the soft carpet of leaves. We hurtled down some tree enclosed tracks in the semi darkness hoping there were no hidden obstacles. The fear is often worse that the obstacle itself so we overcame the fear, replacing it with pure adrenaline. They had named this particular track Paranoia.

It was fantastic to cycle with people whose experience exuded from their riding style. There was a lot I could learn from these guys and it was refreshing to be in such expert company.

After the ride, the For Goodness Shake recovery drink stayed in the car whilst we cracked open a small beer and chatted about riding and stuff. Anne was a bit apprehensive about the World Championships in terms of logistics and costs. I got the impression that she knew there was a lot to organise whilst she was not quite sure where to start. With my love for organising things and wanting to get involved, I offered to do what I could.

Training

The South Downs Triple was not going to ride itself, a serious amount of training and hard work was required. A crazy goal is only achievable with a similar level of dedication and commitment.

By September 2011 training was in full swing. My main riding time was on Saturday mornings where I tried to be home by 1pm. Getting up early I would often leave the house by 7am to get 50-60 miles in before lunch time, whatever the weather. During the rides I didn't take any breaks, it was literally continuous riding for 6 hours. I would load up my pockets and CamelBak with food and drink so I could grab them on the go. Comparing my riding time with my overall time showed that the wheels usually had stopped turning for less than 10 minutes in the whole morning. This was only at road junctions or waiting for horses to pass.

Although Anne was the only person who knew about my aspirations for the Triple, I had a very clear focus on where I was going. I had to find the right people that would help me to get closer to my goal. Looking out for opportunities, I booked myself on to a coaching week with AQR (A Quick Release) in sunny Portugal. Kate and Ian Potter who run AQR have a wealth of knowledge in mountain biking and 24 hour racing at elite and world class levels. They had trained Anne for her World Championships in 2010 so their experience doesn't get much better than this.

During the introductions for the coaching week it was so hard when asked to describe my goals. Giving some vague answer probably implied that I didn't have a goal, which was so untrue. I live by goals, I need a challenge to aspire to and focus my energy. Goals stretch me both mentally and physically and that is how I have been able to develop my cycling at such a pace. The elation of achieving a goal is fantastic as I can tick that one off on my list. There is one goal which has been on my list for a long time, and that is to get on to the podium for a major race. I've often applauded others climbing onto the wooden platforms where they received the accolade they strived to win, and then I would drool over the endless gifts they received in recognition of their achievement. My highest accomplishments were 6th in 24 Hours of Exposure in Scotland and Big Dog in Brighton. Somehow I just couldn't get myself on to the first step of the podium.

In some ways, by setting out to ride the South Downs Triple I was creating my own podium. As long as I became the first person to achieve it, then no one could take that away from me. Secrecy of my intentions at this stage was paramount.

The coaching from AQR was superb, Ian and Kate didn't just tell us how to ride our bikes properly, but covered a whole realm of other aspects to compliment the riding. These included; diet & nutrition, muscle core stability, bike technical set up, fitting the bike to your body, and a VO_2 Max test to measure lung capacity where I surprised myself with a high score.

Up until this point, I had coached myself and it was working well as I was getting stronger, or so I thought. Yes, I was getting stronger, but I had a long way to go if I was to complete the punishing length of the Triple. The 300 miles is a mighty long way where I needed to be really, really fit. It's not just pure fitness but strength in the right areas and not too much muscle bulk where it is not needed.

Enlisting the help of Kate, I made a big and pivotal decision to hand over the training reins. She was a world class champion in 24 hour racing with the experience of endurance riding that I needed.

The first few weeks were hard, very hard, as our training processes clashed. She provided me with what seemed a ridiculous schedule that challenged me mentally. I had to put a lot of trust in Kate, as she was the expert, she got me doing absurd things at funny times of the day. I remember performing endless one legged pedalling routines at 05:30am up and down a quiet road.

Fortunately most of the residents were asleep, so they did not question my sanity.

The main point was efficiency, where I had to ride using a minimum of effort, so I could continue for longer. Other aspects involved 2/3 hour rides before breakfast with only water to drink. These starvation rides built up my ability to burn fats instead of carbs for when the going got tough. (Note: starvation rides should only be undertaken with proper guidance)

Using a turbo trainer where the back wheel of the bike is supported on a resistance wheel, I could train on the stationary bike in a controlled environment. The handle bar display and my Garmin computer showed my pedal speed (cadence), my heart rate (BPM) and the power output (Watts). One exercise involved producing a high power output for 10 minutes followed by a 10 minute warm down and recovery. This process was repeated up to four times where I would really struggle to sustain the increasing power reading for the fourth 10 minute duration. Each 10 minute section would drag as I watched the ticking clock slowly count up the seconds. Mind games were played for distraction and to ease the immense pain. These turbo sessions were tough. I would push myself to the limit to reach her targets, and then she would increase the level for the next week. It was really hard and exhausting, but I focused on the goal and the pain seemed irrelevant.

Although Kate thoroughly tested me mentally and physically, she also provided the practical coaching I needed. Her experience of endurance racing delivered far more than I would have been able to do on my own, making her an integral part of the success of the Triple.

During the peak I was training 20 hours a week, on top of lengthy stretching routines and recovery times. Effective time management was essential to hold down a full time job and care for the family. It was challenging to balance everything in my life, but I had a clear goal and I was determined to achieve it.

The training for each week varied, but generally looked something like this;

Monday	Leg exercises on the bike before work
Tuesday	Leg exercises on the spinners in the gym before work
	Heavy Turbo session in the evening
Wednesday	Swim before work
Thursday	Core Stability exercises or sports massage
Friday	Work in the morning then ride on the South Downs in the afternoon
Saturday	Long ride on the North Downs
Sunday	Day of rest and recovery

From my early cycling days, recording all the statistics and figures for every training session was very important to me. I used a large spread sheet to plan out my schedule noting the different training periods, or phases, and inserted rest weeks. Each session was marked with an objective to define a clear purpose of the training. Each year I added in extra columns and calculations to provide graphical charts of my progress and performance over time. They enabled me to compare year on year results and gauge how well I was doing. I found that to manage something, I needed to start measuring it to focus on the issue. For example, I had to get my weight down, so I weighed myself every week logging the figure on the spread sheet. Knowing that I was getting on the scales each Tuesday evening made me watch what I ate. A graph then showed the trend of my weight, which naturally started coming down.

I also measured my Workload, or RPE (Rating of Perceived Exertion), which is based on Heart Rate and Time during exercise. This enabled me to see how hard my body was working for each session or week of training. Steadily increasing the RPE each week and month provided a gradual build up for my body. I also made sure that every fifth week was a rest week so my body could recover from the intense training. Some purists would say that training should be measured by Power rather than Heart Rate, to which I would agree, however in mountain biking it is difficult to measure Power without a really expensive Power Meter.

One of the areas for mental preparation was to write down all the 'what if' scenarios. If something went wrong or broke, if I crashed badly, if I went off course, if I got attacked by sheep, if the support crew missed me at a check point, if the communications failed, if medically it was unsafe to continue or the worst one, if I didn't complete the Triple. Each situation was carefully worked out and shared with the support crew. This advance preparation provided these advantages;

1. It structured my thinking to provide an outcome that would still be in alignment with my goal.
2. It saved me having to think of a solution whilst on the ride. I could prepare several creative objective options while my mind was fresh and able to function properly. Informing the support crew of the alternative actions in advance enabled them to know what I would do and it allowed them to prepare their response appropriately to the situation.

Mentally and realistically I had to have a plan in case I didn't succeed, as there could always be something that was totally unexpected and catastrophic. I developed a plan in my head, then parked it to one side in the hope that I would never need to retrieve it. Without such a plan and if the worst scenario occurred, I could draw on my preparation to prevent me from disappearing into a chasm of depression and failure. This was the one and only time that I contemplated failure.

With Anne's medical experience, she knew the dangers of riding into extreme exhaustion. At an Olympic training event, she commandeered Dr Jerry Hill on to the support crew to assist. In hindsight, this was one of the best decisions taken. She also did her homework talking to others experienced in ultra-endurance events for advice. I would be riding into a little known area where the medical risks were high, if Anne was going to be a part of it she didn't want to take any chances. She also had the full support of my wife, Fiona, who was equally concerned.

A brief email to Rory Hitchens, the South Downs Double Adjudicator, explaining my intention of the Triple was met with a resounding Yes! Yes! Yes! Encouraging me to go for it.

It was such a relief in May 2012 when I made the announcement. No more secrecy now. Twitter and Facebook exploded; I was not used to such volumes of social media. The comments and questions concerning my sanity arrived in abundance, but this did not deter me, my mind was made up. The challenge was immense and the 3rd June was rapidly approaching, but was I ready?

The Big Day

Friday 1st June 2012

The alarm at 5am caused an interruption to my thoughts. I was already awake and vividly thinking about the day ahead. I had barely slept for more than four hours and there would be no more opportunities to sleep for a very long time, I paused for a final thought before getting out of bed.

Today was the day, the day I had dreamed of for over a year.

Taking a deep breath I got up, showered and donned my ride kit. The thin red dhb Finchdean top with black trims to keep me cool in the hottest of temperatures, black dhb Aeron Race super comfy shorts with red panels, specially purchased red dhb socks to match and my black and red Northwave clean race shoes to complete my set. Later I would add my red and black Giro helmet and red gloves. Oh yes, and the bike is also red and black. There's no superstition, I don't believe in that, I just like everything to match so it all naturally fits together.

Breakfast was a cup of tea and good helping of porridge with a mixture of seeds and nuts sprinkled on top. It was to be my last hot meal for over 50 hours. I tried to eat it slowly but thoughts of what still needed to be done raced around my head as I was gobbling up the last scrapings in the bowl. Light was now evident outside but the house was still silent with the family asleep. I quietly went about preparing the energy drinks for the first few hours of the day. Each 2 litre plastic bottle was made up with 8 scoops of High5 4:1 powder and a Nuun tablet. The formula of carbs with a small amount of protein works for most of my long rides. The Nuun tablet helps to keep the cramps away when I'm sweating a lot. As I was packing the cool box with bottles and ice blocks Simon arrived, momentum was gathering.

We piled the last bits into the Back Pig, which was now pretty full, as Judy appeared. Judy "Beer Babe" and husband Roy dropped everything to help out with the Friday start time. This was only the second occasion we had met and I was delighted that they were prepared to support me.

Back in August 2011 I was watching the rehearsal for the Olympic road race near Box Hill. Talking to a couple next to me about cycling we discovered our shared interest in 24 hour MTB racing and had a number of mutual friends. The couple was Judy and Roy McNeill and we have kept in touch via Twitter since. When Anne contacted them on the Thursday to see if they could help with support on the Friday, they both jumped at the opportunity. Apparently they had planned to come down to see me during my ride, so when they heard about getting fully involved in the challenge they were delighted to be asked.

Roy had to go off to work so Judy, Simon and I headed down to Eastbourne in the rather full Black Pig. I had a sense of excitement and apprehension as we set off down the motorway. Judy studied the ride schedule with the nutritional and clothing requirements and asked lots of questions. She made notes on what I wanted at each check point along with the frequency of the provisions. Gels for every hour, a CamelBak change every 2 hours and a For Goodness Shake every 6 hours etc. As she was taking notes, I wanted to tell her everything, down to the last detail, but I had to focus on the main points. After digesting the first instalment she was ready for more information, taking further meticulous notes. I felt reassured that we both spoke the same language when it came down to detail, which gave me that confidence to leave her to just get on with it.

"Do you have a camera?" She asked.

"Yes, it is in the box marked 'Support Crew Stuff'" I replied as she started to rummage in the box.

"Would you like me to take some pictures for you?"

I was already grateful of Judy's thoughtfulness and this is just want I wanted. So often the support crew get caught up in the technicalities of the race or event and it's not until afterwards that we realise there are no photographs to capture the moments. I thanked Judy for her foresight then checked on Simon that we were going the right way.

The heat of the sun was increasing, giving a feeling that a glorious day lay ahead. Judy was scribbling notes and Simon seemed focused on his driving. I cracked open a For Goodness Shake bottle as part of my pre-ride diet. They are supposed to be recovery drinks but as they are full of carbohydrates, protein and other nutrients, they help me just before and during an endurance ride. As they taste so good they give me something to look forward to every six hours on the ride.

Richard Sterry @hillburner
Driving down to Eastbourne for South Downs Triple, handing Tweets over to support crew, who knows what they might say?

I pointed out to Judy the large file of information for the support crew. It contained maps showing the local 24 hour supermarkets for supplies and the locations of the nearest hospitals. Having this information easily to hand would save valuable time if it was needed. There was a host of other information she could read later that described how to get to each check point and how to mix up my drinks etc.

Just before Eastbourne we made a scheduled stop at a service station so I could lose some ballast from my carbo loading the previous day. The early morning porridge had done its work in my stomach so I could get some movements in my bowels. Who knows when the next time will be when I will see another decent toilet?

Parking in Eastbourne at the start of the South Downs Way I got myself ready. Some of the simple decisions suddenly became difficult as it was now happening for real. What do I wear, arm warmers or bare arms? I put my gloves on then realised I needed sun protection, so the gloves came off. The clock ticked slowly and each minute I thought of something else that perhaps I should do or adjust. In the end I just went for a short ride up the hill to get my legs moving and go for an essential pee.

Nearing the start time of 08:00 I positioned myself by the South Downs Way marker for a photograph. I could feel my heart pounding as I watched the seconds tick by. This was it, it was really happening. I aligned my pedals, looked up the hill and took a deep breath.

There

Eastbourne to Winchester

Friday 1st June 2012 08:00

Why?

That's insane,
I love it.

Go! Shouted Simon and Judy in unison, I turned the pedals and set off up the steep Hill. The new South Downs Way start at Eastbourne delivers a gruelling 300 foot climb at the outset. With only a short warm up this was taken slowly in the granny cog. There was no going back now, the adventure had started and the dream of the Triple 15 months earlier was now becoming a reality.

Crawling up the hill I tried to focus my mind. The past 24 hours had been a complete mayhem with so much to do. I was on my own feeling nervous and apprehensive. I now had to perform. As my nerves started to get the better of me and fill my head with negative thoughts, it dawned on me the enormity of this ride. 300 miles, that's a mighty long way, had I done enough training?

 Judy @beer_babe
At the start of South Downs Way in Eastbourne. @hillburner left at 8am for his triple. Go Richard Go! Let the fun begin! #SD3

Unknown to me at the time a thread about my ride had started on the Singletrack World forum. www.singletrackworld.com

South Downs Way Triple attempt starting shortly

1. **wwaswas**
   Richard Sterry starting out on 300+ miles and more than 30,000ft of climbing at about 8 this morning.
   Been brought forward due to weather forecast for the weekend. @hillburner and hash tag #SD3 on twitter.
   At least the wind's dropped off a bit this morning

2. **weeksy**
   Wow.... that's gonna be a hell of a 30+ hour ride that. !!!

3. **wwaswas**
   'legburner' would be a better twitter name for this ride, I think 🙂

4. **lardman**
   That's very silly.

5. **superfli**

6. **atlaz**
   At what point do we get to question his mental health????
   That's SERIOUSLY impressive

7. **bikebouy**
   Excellent, go for it.

8. **TandemJeremy**
   Why?

9. **allthepies**
   Nutter!

10. **wwaswas**
    Why?
    Because it's there?
    There's a bloke less than 1000km from a world record bicycle circumnavigation. Why? Because he wanted to.
    People doing stuff that I don't understand or want to do myself is not a bad thing in itself is it?

11. **wwaswas**
    progress can be tracked live here (assuming his battery holds out!);
    http://www.endomondo.com/workouts/60289217

12. **TandemJeremy**

wwaswas. I understand doing challenges but riding the same piece of trail 3 times seems odd / lacking in imagination. Why not ride a longer / different trail?

13. **wwaswas**

I guess because in the South East (or maybe England) there aren't that many 300 mile long bits of bridleway that only require the odd road crossing but not much more in the way of tarmac?

Also, it's a progression: SDW in a day was a major challenge for 'early' mtbers, then the double was done and then it was done faster.

It's a recognised route, one that people aspire to ride, setting the 'target' at the next level isn't a bad thing.

My experience of the South Downs is you can ride the same route more than once, but it's never the same twice.

[edit] I think it's one of those things you either 'get' or 'don't get' I'm not going to try and justify someone else's choice of route and personal challenge any further.

14. **njee20**

Does he have a target time?

How long before the first sub 24 triple?!

15. **soma_rich**

TJ, why do the three peaks when you could just go up Everest. FFS the SDW is a known quantity people use the double as a reference to set themselves against others.

16. **muppetWrangler**

I understand doing challenges but riding the same piece of trail 3 times seems odd / lacking in imagination. Why not ride a longer / different trail?

I was kind of thinking along the same lines. The SDW makes sense as a double, but three times does make seem like he's on the wrong route.

It's an impressive ride without a doubt and one he should be proud of but a triple doesn't really capture the imagination.

17. **avdave2**

My experience of the South Downs is you can ride the same route more than once, but it's never the same twice.

I ride on them every day to get to work and then again to get home and I never get bored. 300 miles non stop though does seem like a very tough mental as well as physical challenge.

18. **yesiamtom**

That's insane, I love it. His average speed would suggest 36 hours of riding. Is the Eastbourne bit slow or is this the kind of speed he's gonna pace at the whole ride?

19. **DrP**

wwaswas. I understand doing challenges but riding the same piece of trail 3 times seems odd / lacking in imagination. Why not ride a longer / different trail?

Maybe it's a really long 'bleep test'??

DrP

20. **wwaswas**

9 10 mph is a fairly reasonable average, time, it's a bit lumpy at the Eastbourne end too.

He's aiming for 36 hours ish, I think.

21. **Trimix**

TJ, if you don't get it, don't bother posting on this particular thread. Leave it for those who do get it.

Go and start another one please. With respect, you're not the sort of person who is likely to be persuaded that this is a good challenge / idea 😃

I managed to do only 85 miles of it and that took me 11 hours !

22. **FunkyDunc**

"He's aiming for 36 hours ish, I think."

Is that without stopping for sleep and stuff?

23. **TandemJeremy**

Trimix   au contraire   I get doing "challenges" but merely queried why riding the same bit of trail 3 times was the chosen one here.

24. **richen987**

good luck to him, just doing it one way was challenging enough, shall watch with interest and hope he achieves it.

25. **portlyone**

Not sure I could do 30 miles!

Good luck to the freak man 😊

Simon and Judy opened their first envelope.

Envelope 1 - Eastbourne

This is the first of several envelopes to help you along your way. We are going on a journey to make history and you are as much a part of it as I am. There is no way I can do this without you, so we are doing it together.

Thank you very much for giving up your long weekend and a huge amount of your time to help me. I am honoured to have such a high calibre support crew and really appreciate your assistance.

Your first challenge is to be at the right place at the right time, ensuring you get to the Check Points before me. You may not have driven on the South Downs before, and they are not to be underestimated.

Your second challenge is to keep me riding at a pace where I will complete the 300 miles.

Thirdly, look after yourselves taking breaks when you can, pace yourself as it's going to be a long journey.

Take time to read the support notes so I can whiz in, then whiz out refreshed for the next section.

There are more envelopes to open throughout the day and night and day.

Together we can do it.

Richard

Challenges

I sensed something was wrong

Still on the first hill my legs groaned at the steepness of the climb. Focusing my mind I took time to pray, praying for every part of my body and each aspect of the ride. My deep faith keeps me going with a true purpose in life, so it was only natural that I started with a prayer. I often pray when riding alone and find hill climbing the best time. Armed with a list of people and their situations I had lots to think about on the open hills.

Reaching the top of Warren Hill, barely a mile from the start, I hear hiss, hiss, hiss from the back wheel. "Come on Slime, do your stuff!" The hiss continued as the Slime failed to block up the hole. Crossing the road, I propped the bike up against a post and changed the tube. In my haste, the tyre just would not fit back onto the rim, it was one of those times when you needed 6 hands to hold it in place. I could feel the time slip away, which made me panic even more. Eventually the tyre was sorted with a quick zip of the gas, it was inflated and OK. I'm glad I had the larger 25g gas canisters for the 29er wheels; they worked really well and didn't run out. Back on the bike, I pushed on hard to make up the lengthy 7 minutes of lost time.

My heart rate soared, my head was in a spin and I was puffing like a train. "Get a grip" I told myself, "Calm down." Trying to force my breathing to slow down with deep breaths, my heart continued to pound loudly.

Drastic action was needed; I sat back on the bike, changed down a gear and looked around me. There were some golfers making the most of the fresh morning in the early sunshine. I watched one of them attempt a long putt and heard his shout of delight as the ball disappeared down the hole. That'll be me soon, shouting with delight when I finish my Triple. I wonder what it'll really feel like. Glancing down to my computer, the big number for my heart rate had reduced.

Realising I had no spare tube or patches, and with another 10 miles before my first check point, a second puncture at this time could be disastrous. Riding carefully on the track across the golf course, I stayed on the grass to avoid any sharp stones or flints. It was also time to pray for the bike, I had omitted this previously, where now seemed the appropriate moment.

The descents were fast so I deliberately took it easy, a mistake at such an early stage would be a tad embarrassing.

Climbing in the shadow of the trees after passing the church at Jevington my legs gobbled up the trail. They had warmed up and made light of the incline. It was important to pace myself so I did not burn out too quickly. Picking a smooth line over the lumpy hardened mud that had been shaped by horses' hooves wasn't easy; I picked my way forward occasionally raising the front wheel up and over the protruding roots.

Back into the sunlight I picked up momentum as I could see the vast open spaces with steep drops into the valleys either side. The rolling hills stretched out before me as I looked across to the radio masts near Firle. Passing the occasional sheep and with the wind cooling my face, my speed steadily increased.

After dropping into Alfriston, the first check point was at Firle car park. I love this place; it's on the top of a hill with beautiful views all around. Having just passed Firle Beacon, there was a gentle descent to the car park above the village of Firle. Changing into the big ring I glided across the field and watched my speed increase. As I approached from the distance Simon and Judy were waiting expectantly for me like parents meeting their child after his first day at school.

"I need a tube" I shouted. Simon started rummaging in the drawers for a spare tube. We had 2 sets of 4 drawers containing all the bits of kit, but in our haste to start the ride early nothing was labelled. He found a tube and also gave me some patches, just in case further disasters struck.

The van was packed with kit to cover virtually any eventuality; amongst loads of food, clothing, medical bits, tools, bike bits and a spare bike there was a small space for the support crew and their provisions. During the previous months a small fortune had been spent taking advantage of special offers from on-line bike stores to gather all the contents of the planned kit list. I made sure there was at least two of everything with options for different conditions.

An equipment list is essential for this sort of ride. Being an organised chap with a love of spread sheets, I had everything tabulated. It helped me to focus on what I really needed so the kitchen sink could be left behind whilst it enabled me to remember to pack enough spare batteries for all the gadgets that might need replacements. It took a long time to compile such a list so I started it early on in the project. When the special offers and sales appeared, I knew exactly what I wanted so bought it at the best price.

The spare bike was my trusty Specilaized S-Works M5 hard-tail. As the wheels were 26" with Schrader valves whilst the main bike was a 29er with Presta valves, I had colour coded everything in my meticulous preparation. Blue tape marked the special items for the spare bike and red tape for the main bike. The multi-tool containing a chain splitter had a couple of Quick Links taped to it for speedy chain repairs. As the main bike has a 10 speed cassette and the spare bike a 9 speed cassette, the chain Quick Links are slightly different. I therefore had two multi-tools each with the different Quick Links fixed with the appropriate colour tape. The spare tubes and tyres were also colour coded accordingly. This may all sound a bit nerdy but it saves time and avoids confusion with the wrong bits. Even the track pump had red and blue tape on the valve nozzles to show which is which.

Judy @beer_babe

#SD3 @hillburner **just made a rapid transition through CP1 having had 1st puncture en-route. Go Richard Go and keep smiling.**

Setting off from Firle towards the radio masts I prepared myself for the descent to the A26 and the River Ouse. The first time I rode down here, it was scary. It's like going down in a roller coaster where you can't see the track that will get you to the bottom. The hill gets steeper and steeper with speed rising above 30mph, yet I still couldn't see the entire track. As the curve lessens, the track becomes visible, leading the way down the hill. I rode this descent braking as late as possible, if at all, to get the maximum grin factor.

Part way down the chalk track on the lower section there is a gate that disrupts all momentum and sense of speed. Slamming the gate shut behind me, I continued down the track. It curves tightly round to the left where there is a humped backed bridge at Itford Farm going over the A26. I like to see how much speed I can carry down the track and round the corner to be able to freewheel over the hump of the bridge. It's a sad game to play, but when you are on your own for hours on end, it's these little things that keep you going.

Since riding the South Downs Triple I've discovered others who play similar games on this section of the trail. Perhaps we are all as mad as each other.

26. **soma_rich**
Only hit 24mph going down South Ease

27. **miketually**
Good luck to him. I'll be watching and (virtual) cheering online.

I like these things. Mike Hall's almost home, Tour Divide (Fixie dave Nice is already ITTing it from South to North) kicks off soon and Aidan's EWE race is next month.

28. **jam bo**
Trimix   au contraire   I get doing "challenges" but merely queried why riding the same bit of trail 3 times was the chosen one here.
You've done a 24 hr event before?

29. **pedalhead**

Good luck to him. Anybody know how many gates that'll be?

30. **muggomagic**

Why do it 3 times?

I would guess it's because it's going one better than what been done before. I don't doubt in years to come that someone will do the double double. It's what people do always strive to go one better than what has been done before.

31. **FunkyDunc**

Who's going to do the battery pit stop for his phone, or is it some other device tracking him.

The run at the start of May was quite an impressive time! Although he quite obviously has a thing for doing dull routes ie repeating the same trail.

32. **IanMunro**

you've done a 24 hr event before?

Yeah, they're daft too
I get TJ's point.
Richard's ride is going to be really impressive in athletic achievement, but to me, and really want to emphasises the 'me' bit, isn't very inspirational. But as it's not his purpose in life to inspire me, that's not meant as a complaint in any form and I hat's off to him attempting it!!
I guess it reminds me of people who do an Ironman, then a double ironman, then a triple, then a decca. It seems like going on holiday to the same place each year but for longer.
Which is also fine.

33. **surfer**

Daisy Duke off here did a double last year. He was hoping for a sub 24 but a couple of tumbles and a problem with his lights meant he missed it by about an hour IIRC.

Top effort though

34. **muppetWrangler**
    It seems like going on holiday to the same place each year but for longer.
    My sister does that and she is definitely weird.

35. **Paceman**
    Full respect to him, it may not be the most interesting terrain etc and doing it three times over seems insane, but as others have said, he's 300 miles away from a world mountain biking first record which is an achievement in my opinion.

    I'm in Worthing and it's warm and humid out there right now... he's going to need to drink plenty over the next 36hrs that's for sure.

    Loving the fact he has a live progress feed! Very clever.
    http://www.endomondo.com/workouts/60289217

36. **wwaswas**
    My sister does that and she is definitely weird.
    It's probably genetic 😊

37. **muppetWrangler**
    It's probably genetic 😟

38. **portlyone**
    Cheer up, you might be adopted

39. **wwaswas**
    Cheer up, you might be adopted
    That could make a good nature or nurture type study 😊

40. **DrP**
    Currently tracking him too.
    I might go and nick his bike and phone when he next comes past me.... (Actually, I'll get him third time round bound to be less of a fight...)
    DrP

41. jimification

That must be near 300 gates! (unless he's lucky with cooperative ramblers)

Muggomagic: Yes, he's already done a double and the double record is very fast...on another double he'd be competing with the likes of Ian Leitch and Josh Ibbett to set a new record. No one's done the triple yet, though and the record is there for the taking and I guess it's a bit more noteworthy than another "slower" double.

Good luck to him anyway. I'm out on the downs myself today and tomorrow and will keep an eye out for him.

42. longwayhome

I'm with TJ (Oh my God!) and muppetWrangler on this.

Why do it 3 times?

I would guess it's because it's going one better than what been done before. I don't doubt in years to come that someone will do the double double. It's what people do always strive to go one better than what has been done before.

muggomagic

After a double where does it end? Five times back to back? Ten times? A hundred times?

Will anyone care if you manage 25 times when the previous record was 24 etc. etc. and is 25 times in 15 days more or less of an achievement than 24 times in 13 days?

Leave it at 2!

TJ, why do the three peaks when you could just go up Everest.

soma_rich

Exactly TJ's point   both of those are just one "lap" with no repetition.

43. miketually

As a natural thing to aim for, "there and back" does make more sense than "there and back and there again".

44. **grazedknees**

All challenges have a different spin. This is undoubtedly a physical challenge but also a massive psychological challenge. To do one lap or A to B keeps you motivated but to reach the 'end' after 24 hours and then turn back again?!

45. **miketually**

As a first go at riding for much more than 24 hours, doing it on familiar terrain makes sense.

46. **muppetWrangler**

Cheer up, you might be adopted

I've often thought that was the pretty likely, seemed rude to ask though.

Some of the comments do get a little side tracked and there certainly are mixed feelings about my ride. There's a distinct difference between those who know the South Downs and have ridden the full length, compared to those who think the South Downs Way is gentle meandering bridleway.

For this sort of distance I would rather ride on familiar trails and the South Downs Way is one of the longest bridleways in the country. The beautiful surroundings also make it a great couple of days out on the bike.

Seeing the green pedestrian light I crossed over the railway line followed by the bridge over the River Ouse. Once on the short road section I took the opportunity to down an energy gel. Packed with carbohydrates and sugars the gloopy stuff from the sachet slides down easily followed by a quick drink of water. Some people don't like the taste or texture, but considering them as a necessity to sustain energy, makes them more palatable. Using the Torq range, my favourite is the Bannoffee Pie flavour. One of the things about endurance riding is the weird cravings for bizarre food. I had asked each person in the support crew to bring along something that they thought I might like later in the ride. There's nothing worse than a massive desire for a speciality and not having the food available.

After an awkward descent with a gate half way down, then a stupidly steep climb by a smelly farm, I was back in the open fields with the sheep. The sheep are funny animals and somewhat more jumpy than the docile cows. It's always better to warn the sheep well in advance of your arrival, so they can search for their brain cell, then work out which way to go. If they don't hear or see you until the last minute, they could jump anywhere, which may be towards you. They don't take kindly to 'Baa' or other sheep impersonations; instead a sharp 'Hiss' usually wakes them up.

Climbing the long concrete road soon after Rodmell I sensed something was wrong. My pedalling was OK, but the back of the bike was flexing a bit too much. I didn't want to stop to check the tyre pressure, so thought and worried about what else could be causing the instability. Would I need to use my spare bike at this early stage? Reaching the gate at the top I eventually stopped to feel the tyre, it was soft. Not wanting to change the tube, I grabbed the gas inflator from my back pocket and zapped some more air into it. Checking that it was nice and firm, I continued along the top of the ridge, hoping that it would stay up.

The clear blue sky and the warm sun provided all the ingredients for a glorious day. I had made the right decision not to wear anything on my arms. Pushing on along the ridge, I admired the views over Lewes to my right and the sea to my left. This is my favourite part of the South Downs Way being on top of the ridge following the natural undulations of the hills. The route of the South Downs Way is sparsely marked by the finger posts and blue acorn signs. This is fine in good light if you know where you are going, but in darkness or poor visibility it can be quite challenging to navigate across the open fields where the gate on the other side cannot be seen. This was one of the factors when deciding on a start time for the ride, I arranged for the parts in darkness to be on well-defined bridleways to reduce navigational errors.

There's something wonderful about riding on your own in such an open space. It's just you and your bike; no other interferences, worries or distractions. Call it a form of escapism, a way to de-stress and leave all your worries behind. I have a strict rule when riding alone; I am not allowed to think about work. Once I start, the pressures quickly build up about what is happening in the office and all the things that need to be done fill my mind.

I heard an unfamiliar rattle. My heart sank as the fear of further disasters entered my mind. Stopping again, I saw that the saddle pouch was open and the one and only spare tube had fallen out. This ride wasn't going well. Checking in vain behind me for the escaped tube, the only comfort was that my newly purchased multi-tool was still in the pouch. I zipped it up and carried on. Whatever could happen next?

Thinking about my ride I contemplated how lucky I was to be able to do what I love doing all day, then all night, and then for the whole of the next day. There was no pressure to be back home by a certain time, it was just me, the bike and the South Downs Way.

I was very conscious at this point that I had no spare tube (again) so stayed on the grass wherever possible. Descending down to the A27 felt good. The air rushed past as the speed increased and all too soon I was in the narrow section negotiating the five gates in quick succession before the road.

Glancing across the dual carriage way, Simon and Judy were sitting comfortably in chairs on the grass enjoying the sunshine as if they had all the time in the world. Once over the bridge, they were ready for action with whatever I needed.

"Another tube please" I called to Simon and saw his smirk turn into concern, realising that I might have had another puncture. Judy topped up my back pocket with energy gels as I was handed a replacement CamelBak. Within a minute the wheels were rolling again as I was on my way. I don't like long pit stops; we exchange the essential information, I receive my supplies and then I get going.

The refuelling strategy was relatively straight forward. Every couple of hours I would swap to a different CamelBak back pack that was prefilled with energy drink that I drank from a tube. This enabled the support crew to mix the drinks and prepare the spare CamelBaks in advance. I used 3 CamelBak Classics, each of a different colour so we knew which was which. The first two were for the High5 4:1 drink and the third contained Torq drink when I fancied a change. I also carried 3 gels in my back left pocket and I tried to take one every hour on the hour. The centre pocket was used for rubbish while the right pocked contained any non-food items. In addition, I had a small pouch by the stem at the front with chopped up energy bars and flapjack pieces to nibble. For such a long ride it is essential to have variety in both the flavour and the texture of food.

Judy @beer_babe
#SD3 @hillburner **spent 2 minutes at CP2, just off A27. Average up to 9.2mph & I think we got a smile from him! Go Richard Go! Open envelope.**

Judy @beer_babe
#SD3 **Envelope opened. Got to make paper planes! Thanks** @hillburner ;-)

Judy @beer_babe
#SD3 @hillburner **has an evil streak in him. Neither** @dadwithabike **or I can make his paper plane. He's on his own now!! Only joking!** ;-)

Motivation

I was behind schedule

There's an awkward climb up from the A27 followed by a stupid descent at Bunkershill Plantation. It is a very steep slope where all the effort in climbing the hill is all lost in a very short time. I don't mind climbing hills as long as there is a decent descent afterwards where I can gain some distance at a good speed. Controlling my downward movement with careful positioning on the bike and coordination of the front and rear brakes to prevent skidding, to me on this sort of ride, is just a waste of potential energy.

The next part is a long gradual climb across the fields at Balmer Down before you get to the ridge at Plumpton Plain. It was time to turn on the iPod to ease the monotony of the hills. There's a whole concoction of music that I listen to, it's all upbeat motivational stuff that keeps me going. The variety is immense; from heavy rock to new romantics, and from TV theme tunes to Soul Survivor classics. Every song carries a memory to somewhere in my past, so I have plenty to think about on the ride.

Crossing the road at Ditchling Beacon always brings back memories of the London to Brighton rides I first did as a teenager. I enjoyed the freedom of cycling as a kid and chose to do the Duke of Edinburgh expedition by bike instead of walking. Occasionally I rode the 50 miles home from boarding school near Maidstone when we were allowed out for the weekend. As a fifteen year old this was pretty adventurous. My parents trusted and supported me in getting out doing things for myself. Perhaps this is where I'm happy to attempt something outside my comfort zone and take on challenges that have not been tried before.

Once I learnt to drive, the bike gathered dust in the shed for the next 15 years. I was never interested in sport or doing exercise,

I couldn't see the point and I certainly wasn't motivated to do anything about it. My older brother Dave was the sporty one; he spent 12 years in the Royal Engineers and was far more active than the rest of the family put together.

There is however one exception in the family who was sporty, and that was my Great Grandmother. Charlotte Cooper, later Mrs Alfred Sterry, was a tennis player. She won the Wimbledon ladies singles 5 times between 1895 and 1908 and became the first female Olympic champion in the 1900 Olympic Games. She won Gold Medals in the Ladies Singles and the Mixed Doubles. It was an honour to go to the Olympic Museum in August 2012 to see her achievements celebrated alongside Sir Steve Redgrave, Dame Kelly Holmes and 13 other Olympic champions.

Charlotte Cooper
1870-1966

Back in 2002 the management team at work was told to attend a motivational training course. I really didn't want to go and had far too much to do, but reluctantly turned up because all the other managers were going. If there's ever a time when my life completely changed, it was during the next three days. Ben Hunt-Davis who won Gold in the 2000 Sydney Olympics for rowing, showed me that I had a choice in everything. I could take control of my thoughts, my emotions, my actions and ultimately my results. This became incredibly empowering to direct my life rather than let it wander due to the influences of others.

Having sat on my backside for 15 years doing no exercise and piling on the pounds, I set a goal to get fit. Aiming for the London to Brighton bike ride I wanted to see if I could match the 4:30 hours it took me several years previously. Using the 20 year old bike I had as a teenager, I stormed into Brighton in just 3:20 hours. What a result, I felt fantastic. I felt I had really achieved something. Mountain biking appealed to me much more than road cycling, so I forked out what I thought was a lot of money for my first MTB, costing £180. Riding it every week the bike only lasted a year before it had to be replaced. Setting bigger goals every year has challenged and inspired me to do more.

Within a couple of years I completed the London to Brighton in just 2:57 hours beating my 3 hour target. It was on the same old road bike so there were no advantages of modern technology. Again I felt fantastic.

Turning back to the frustrations on the first part of the Triple ride, they could have been the beginning of the end. Choosing to focus on the outcome in overcoming the setbacks kept me going. It is not what happens to us but our reaction to the situation that determines the outcome. Choosing our reaction carefully makes a dramatic difference to the end result. As Ben taught me to say;

'Today is going to be a good day,
because **I** am going to make it a good day.'

During my working career I've been faced with redundancy twice. Each time I was determined to make the most of the opportunities and came out stronger than before. It all comes down to your attitude which is based on your pattern of beliefs. Taking appropriate actions I was able to spot the possibilities and climb the career ladder.

Chris Harding @The_Kraken
#sd3 @hillburner's about to start the punishing climb up Newtimber Hill, for the 1st time. I hate that climb so much.

Back to my ride, I descended towards the A23 with my speed picking up but my average was still lower than planned. I had a long way to go and I was behind schedule. Keeping it steady, I crossed over the A23 and climbed the gritty Newtimber Hill to Saddlescombe.

Stopping briefly, I grabbed a wrap as part of my real food diet. Honey, marmite or marmalade spread across a wrap, then rolled up into a sausage, provides an easy to eat carbo boost with a sweetener. Chopping the wrap in half lets it fit neatly into the pouch on the bike stem for convenience. Although I didn't feel hungry, I had to eat to keep up the energy levels. Eating these measured amounts little and often enabled my stomach to steadily process the food.

Judy @beer_babe
#SD3 @hillburner **has headed out of CP3 maintaining a 9.1mph average. Still has a smile on his face (or is it a grimace)**

Climbing up to Devil's Dyke, the bridleway is on the top of the ridge providing more spectacular views in all directions. Changing the start to the Friday meant that the undulating trails were beautifully clear and free from others enjoying the scenery at perhaps a different speed. Approaching the bottom of one of the dips near Fulking is where I met my first group of cyclists. There's a gate at the base of the valley and my timing was perfect. The 4 guys kitted out in colourful waterproofs started climbing up to Truleigh Hill. Riding with them for a few moments they said they were going all the way to Winchester. These guys looked as though they had the determination to see it through. They had set off early from Eastbourne and were kitted out for a full days ride. Asking me how far I was going, I told them. "There and back, then there again." I'm not sure if they believed my answer, so I wished them well and headed up to the top of the hill.

47. **cakefest**
Why not do the SDW triple? FFS plenty of people get paid millions for riding/running round and round the same tracks again and again.
Respect to the long distance lunatics.

48. **IanMunro**
Loving the fact he has a live progress feed! Very clever.
http://www.endomondo.com/workouts/60289217
Just looked at his feed   ran 37 miles on the SDW at 6:12 min/mile.
Eeek!

49. **longwayhome**
Why not do the SDW triple? FFS plenty of people get paid millions for riding/running round and round the same tracks again and again.
cakefest
Yes, but you don't get everyone doing Mayhem or the World Championships turning it into a challenge, having a website to track their progress and starting a thread on here.
Respect to the long distance lunatics.
cakefest
Yes, but chose a longer route rather than do one multiple times.

50. **wwaswas**
To be fair the bloke doing it didn't start the thread, I did, and lots of people start Mayhem threads on here...
I'm not sure what he's doing is any 'worse' than a race on a circuit that people do multiple times in 24 hours etc, he just has 100 mile 'laps' not 20 mile ones?

51. **ChrisE**

If you were going to ride as far as that, would you not find somewhere a bit better, bit nicer, to ride, ie not southern England!!

52. **monksie**

I love this kind of stuff, more so because it's on the same route repeated.
I know he won't have the slightest inkling of this but I wish him the very best in his attempt. It's a tough day out doing it in one direction.
Go on fella!

53. **miketually**

I'm not sure what he's doing is any 'worse' than a race on a circuit that people do multiple times in 24 hours etc, he just has 100 mile 'laps' not 20 mile ones?

Exactly. Instead of trying to do as many laps as possible in a set time, he's trying to do three laps as fast as possible.

54. **longwayhome**

Nobody has addressed my question.
Where do you stop?

55. **monksie**

Doing the route more than once in the same ride adds to the challenge. A significant part of this is mental.
I'm riding London to Manchester in 13 hours (I hope) in July. Toward the end of it, I know I'll be struggling but being able to focus on the distance going past and knowing I won't have to look at it (the same bit of road) again will help. A small but very helpful mental stimulus. Imagine being knackered **and** knowing you have to do the same thing again. You really have to dig mentally deep when you're wiped out and it's the same scenery.

56. **Herman Shake**

What a beast! Looks like he's on big wheels too.
Maybe the next thing is the SDW3 on a fatty? There must be loads of records to be grabbed on a chubster.

57. **surfer**

> *Nobody has addressed my question.*
>
> *Where do you stop?*

Its not a very good question however you don't stop. If he breaks/creates a record for 3 then its there to be beaten.

58. **CaptJon**

> *TandemJeremy*
>
> *Trimix   au contraire   I get doing "challenges" but merely queried why riding the same bit of trail 3 times was the chosen one here*

"same bit of trail" makes it sound like he's sessioning a short part all day, not cycling 300 miles off road!

59. **m1kea**

> *surfer*
>
> *Daisy Duke off here did a double last year. He was hoping for a sub 24 but 7 punctures in the first 50 miles a ~~couple of tumbles and a problem with his lights~~ meant he missed it by about an hour IIRC.*
>
> *Top effort though*
>
> FTFY

By complete chance I caught Ben that day at about 60 miles. I'd taken 1:40 out of him as we climbed to Truleigh Hill and I was well impressed to read that he had the chops to carry on to finish. I would have certainly bailed well before then.

Very best of luck to Richard and I sincerely hope he makes it. My best double attempt failed at 15 hours and it is all about the mental will to carry on.

I completely get why he's trying the triple.

60. **bennyboy1**

Good luck to him, wish him all the best for this massive challenge.

61. **cakefest**

   Chris E   If you were going to ride as far as that, would you not find somewhere a bit better, bit nicer, to ride, ie not southern England!!

   Don't think it's got anything to do with the scenery. Except for the first chunk of miles and then blips along the way. I think the SDW is virtually a motorway   technically not too tricky when dry   and built for this sort of long distance effort.

   Longwayhome   Nobody has addressed my question. Where do you stop?

   Incredible question. How did we get aeroplanes? Gunpowder? Oil? Flasks? Battenburg cake? Printing press?

   You never, ever stop.

62. **FunkyDunc**

   Whats the record one way?

63. **Aidan**

   Good luck to him, it's going to be tough.

   To those who are grumbling about a 3 way (ha!), the only reason to ever care what other people think about your challenges is if you are sponsored up to the eyeballs and/or a career adventurer.

   Guys like this get more respect from me, they do it because they want to.

64. **avdave2**

   Richard Sterry was out running. He tracked 36.87 mi in 3h:48m:37s.

   This is from his profile on the link   he may be mad!

65. **Mostly Balanced**

   I'm just jealous of him having enough spare time to seriously train for and attempt something like that.

66. **DrP**

   Begrudgingly, I agree....
   DrP

67. **trb**

I wish him luck, it's a seriously tough challenge and the only SDW x 3 challenge I'm ever likely to do is 1 way in 3 days!

But........ I'm with TJ, 3 times? I just don't get it.

68. **Cheezpleez**

Can't believe all the people carping about whether this is a valid challenge. FFS!

If you don't like it, either just ignore it or go and do something more impressive/imaginative.

Like my dear old mum used to say: if you've got nothing positive to say, don't say anything.

69. **jameso**

I'm really surprised people are asking 'why'.. Inspiring stuff imo, I can't imagine how tough the 2nd turn around must be.

70. **IanMunro**

Like my dear old mum used to say: if you've got nothing positive to say, don't say anything.

And whining about people who have differing opinions to you is positive how?

Detail

*Nothing was going to stop me
and I wanted this moment to last for ever.*

Using the smooth road down from Truleigh Hill, I grabbed another gel. It's easiest to open the gels with two hands so riding without holding the handle bars is essential to be able to eat on the go. There are not many road sections on the South Downs Way but with careful planning they were used to my advantage. I was eating and drinking well but the pressure was on to get to Winchester by 7pm.

Passing the small car park at the end of the road reminded me of the MaXx Exposure Ride organised by Trail Break. They mark out the South Downs Way route so riders can cover 80 miles from Eastbourne to the QECP in the dark. One of the check points for their ride is at this small car park at Beeding Hill.

In my early cycling days I participated in many of the Trail Break events where you can follow the marked out route at your own pace. There was a small group of us from Redhill Cycling Club consisting of Garry Hall, Alex Bottomley, Dave Ricketts and David Peacock. Each month we would drive to the chosen location and enjoy riding in a new area. I remember a significant step we took to move up from the Standard 25 mile route to the Long 35 mile route. It felt like an epic journey to ride 35 miles.

Much of my riding at this time was with Redhill Cycling Club where Garry Hall and I grew and developed the MTB section of the club. 'Captain Garry' was the Gung Ho leader happy to be out in front, where I focused on the detail and logistics to make it all happen. We worked well together providing a variety of rides for the club members, often planning events over a curry. Garry was also a great friend as we often rode together exploring new trails.

We organised trips to Wales twice a year attracting 15 to 30 like-minded members for a fun packed, often muddy, weekend.

In 2008 I noticed that Trail Break was not running its regular ride at Gatwick, so I contacted Martin and Phil Harrison to see if we could help set up a local ride on the North Downs. After finding a suitable location to use as a base I put together the MTB routes to create their Reigate event. In later years this annual item on their calendar enables me to give something back as I usually find myself helping out in one way or another.

There's a long climb up past Steyning Bowl to Chanctonbury Ring, it's not too steep but you need to concentrate so your speed doesn't drop too much. The views again are wonderful with great open spaces and I was in my own little world enjoying the moment with the iPod thumping away.

"Are you Richard?" asked a voice that appeared from nowhere. Somewhat surprised to see another cyclist and someone asking my name, I said that I was. He introduced himself as Jim Russell saying that he had been following me on my Endomondo GPS tracker. The live tracker showed my location on a web site where the link had been tweeted out. Jim was heading out for a ride and decided to see if he could find me.

We chatted for a few minutes about the joys of cycling and 29er bikes before he went on ahead to inform the support crew of my imminent arrival. It was nice to have some company as I had been riding alone for about 4 hours.

Jim was not the only person watching the Endomondo tracker. Apparently the word was spreading rapidly with many people glued to their screen watching the dot slowly move. Another feature of the tracker is the Pep Talk. Simon was logged into Endomondo on his iPad to monitor my progress where he could type in a message. The message was then verbally read out to me as I rode along. Taking turns to entertain me the support crew passed on a few words of encouragement and messages to keep me going.

There was also a safety aspect for the tracker. If I failed to turn up at a check point, the support crew would be able to see where I had stopped or if I had already passed that check point. Riding alone in remote areas for long durations carries its risks, which increase at night time.

> June 01 at 12:35 - Simon says "We are at the check point, where are you?"

Judy closely monitored Twitter, passing on messages and tweeting with feedback. It was so uplifting to hear words of support from other endurance riders.

use-exposure @use_exposure
Follow @use_exposure supported rider @hillburner on his South Downs Triple attempt here:
http://www.endomondo.com/workouts/60289217

Chris Harding @The_Kraken
#FF @hillburner he started the Triple South Downs Way. That's Eastbourne to Winchester, then back, then to Winchester again. Amazing! #sd3

Stopping briefly at Washington, I spoke to Anne on the phone who was about to head out to join us. Giving her some detailed instructions, I asked her to pop by my house to collect my muddy, tatty old cycling shoes.

There was a pain in my right knee, it didn't feel right and at this early stage if it wasn't sorted out it would only get worse. I had set out in my nice clean race shoes with the red flecks to blend in with my black and red colour scheme for myself and the bike. They looked great, but I felt they could be the cause of my knee problem, possibly due to the cleat alignment on the shoe. Swapping to a relatively new pair of shoes the knee pain quickly disappeared, but the soles of my feet began hurting. The red dhb socks matched my red and black theme by they were much thinner than my normal riding socks. Putting on a thicker pair at Washington, I also took the opportunity to ask Anne to bring down my old favourite shoes. Sometimes you just have to go for comfort rather than looks.

The A24 was clear of traffic as Jim and I crossed over the dual carriage way and climbed up the other side. It was certainly warm as we rode along the ridge admiring the views. For one brief moment I thought about the guys at work, and then felt so much better for being out in the open air doing something I love.

Soon I was heading down Amberley Rise, quite a steep descent, then crossing over the River Arun. Checking the route out a few weeks previously, the thick mud on the embankment by the bridge was virtually unrideable due to the heavy rain. Progress on the recce ride was slow and I wondered how I would be feeling doing the real thing. I do a lot of visualisations and imagined myself powering up a climb or bombing down a descent. The reality of the mud infested trails at this time made the going really tough, so covering 300 miles in those conditions would be extremely difficult. It was therefore essential to get a good weather window for the big ride.

The earlier week of baking sunshine had now hardened the mud making it so much easier to ride, if not a bit bumpy on my hard-tail bike. In fact all the trails were now bone dry and super-fast.

My bike was a carbon Scott Scale hard tail with 29" wheels. I wanted a lightweight bike that would cruise effortlessly along the bridleways. Previously I had built up my own bikes to my exact requirements but this time I bought one off the shelf. A big consideration for me was the gear ratios and how they compared to my 26" wheeled bikes. Some would say 'rather sadly' but I consider it as 'being thorough', I created a spread sheet to do all the calculations to compare the gear ratios for the different gear set ups for 26" and 29" bikes. Using this and other information enabled me to select the Scott Scale with its 3 x 10 gearing.

Full suspension bikes are often heavier and can become less efficient when pedalling up hills. Hill climbing is one of my cycling strengths, which I partly put down to the hard tail bike. I realised some years ago that most riders dislike the big hills and they are the main time consumers when racing. Concentrating on hill climbing techniques and riding many hills in succession during training rides, I significantly improved my overall performance. Gaining a reputation for being a bit of a mountain goat, my Twitter name is appropriately @HillBurner.

Tyre choice for the bike was easy; the Kenda Small Block 8s provided little drag and rolled incredibly well on the firm and dry trails. I had used these tyres for my South Downs Double and had every confidence in them for the Triple. Complete trust in your tyres and knowing how much you can push them when braking and cornering is essential. When racing I usually have a spare set of wheels with different tyres for wetter conditions. This provides the flexibility and choice if the weather changes.

Climbing up to the road at Bury Hill I saw the familiar faces of the support crew who replaced my CamelBak and topped up my pockets with gels. They had certainly got themselves into a routine by this stage so the stops were very brief and functional. I think this is where Jim departed. He kindly acknowledged that this was intended to be a solo ride and had kept slightly behind me. I tend to bury myself in my thoughts on a long ride so wasn't very talkative. It was reassuring to have someone near me and I really appreciated him taking the time to come and find me. Thanks Jim.

Leaving Bury there is a steep climb up Bignor Hill, then over to Gatting Beacon before a descent to Littleton Farm. There is an abundance of evidence left behind from cows around this farm where it gets my vote for the smelliest farm on the South Downs Way. Climbing up to Graffam Down it is slightly flatter as I headed towards Cocking.

The few gates I came across on this section were flicked open whilst my feet were still clipped into the pedals. It took me a while to perfect the art of smooth gate opening where it saves time when getting through them. It's a matter of approaching the gate at an angle from the hinge side; reaching over the handlebars for the gate leaver and nudging the gate open with the front wheel. As the gate opens move forward and swing the gate shut as you propel yourself off. Usually a click can be heard as the latch closes. If there is livestock in the field a quick glance back to check the gate is properly fastened helps to keep the farmers happy. In 2007 I counted 96 gates along the whole route, much to the annoyance of Garry who was riding with me. Other people have also reached a similar figure. Along with seasonal variations and a few extras on the Temporary route by Exton there are pretty much 100 gates in all. Therefore for the Triple I had 300 gates to negotiate. That's a lot of opening and closing, so efficiency was the key.

The 29er wheels gobbled up the trails as I cruised effortlessly along with the wind rushing past. This felt so good; it's what riding is all about. My legs were really performing well and the average speed was increasing. Nothing was going to stop me and I wanted this moment to last for ever. How often can you do what you really enjoy doing all day? Downing another gel I descend past the tap to Cocking.

Surprised not to see the support crew at the car park, I simply followed the procedure for a missed check point and went on. 500 metres up the track, I saw the Black Pig with Simon and Judy waiting patiently for me. They had decided to create their own location for the check point. However much you plan and organise an event, sometimes you just have to go with the flow.

Tucking into another prepared wrap, I'm handed a fresh CamelBak and headed up the 300 foot climb for the next 2 miles. It is very easy to lose speed and motivation on a long climb so I make sure there is some good music on the iPod or I have something solid to think about. Using this distraction and sustaining a good rhythm with my legs, the hill soon vanishes. On tougher climbs I find myself counting the most ridiculous things to occupy my mind. These can include fence posts, trees, mole hills or anything that I pass on the way.

71. Trimix

Just looked at his progress at this rate he will need 25,532 calories by the time he has finished.

Almost 10 times the amount we should normally eat.

That will be some massive curry/beer fest at the end then 😃

72. large418

I get why he's doing this. It's a challenge that he's set himself doesn't matter that it's the SDW it could be any epic route. Top respect from here.

There's a huge number of people who don't get why we ride bikes. Doesn't make it bad or wrong, just different. I love the fact that there are some people out there who want to push the boundaries of what is possible.

25,000 calories that's like eating a fat person!

73. Cheezpleez

@IanMunro Fair cop. I thought that myself after I posted it 😃

Just think it's incredible that the only thing people can think of to say about this guy's effort is that it's a bit unimaginative or somehow wrong.

Good luck to him!

74. Trimix

Eating 25,000 calories would be tough enough !

75. weeksy

Trimix
Eating 25,000 calories would be tough enough !
Oh i dunno.. sounds like a decent weekend to me.

76. IanMunro

Just think it's incredible that the only thing people can think of to say about this guy's effort is that it's a bit unimaginative or somehow wrong.

Good luck to him!

No worries, I know exactly what you meant, I was just being an arse 😃

Talking of which hopefully they're won't be any pics of his after 36 hours 😬

77. **miketually**
    You can't eat 25000 calories in 36 hours.
    If he eats 60g of carbs per hour, that's 8640 calories. Even if he's trained himself to eat more carbs than that, it'll not be enough. He'll be running on body fat.
    5000 calories = 6.25 pounds of fat

78. **wwaswas**
    25000 calories = 6.25 pounds of fat
    let's hope he's not a scrawny bugger with no fat   he'll be bonking badly by the end.

79. **bikebouy**
    Anyone know where he is now?
    I can't access his data from That Work Thing.
    What bikes he on too??

80. **chiefgrooveguru**
    Seeing that feed I'm quite tempted to join him for a few miles as he passes Brighton again!

81. **wwaswas**
    Cocking Hill. Not sure what bike.

82. **chiefgrooveguru**
    He's just crossing the Midhurst road

the Real BeerBiker @BeerBiker
7 Hours in and @hillburner is slogging it out on the long drag that is Cocking Hill, 36 miles to Winchester
http://www.endomondo.com/workouts/60289217

John McFaul @JohnMcFaul
Gutted I can't cheer @hillburner on as he passes Cocking for the 1st time. I know how much a cheer, chat or nod can make a difference #sd3

Rob Lee @RobLee7ds
@hillburner **good pace so far. How are you feeling?**
Keep on, keeping on

Sean Skinner @SeanUSX
I am amazed at @hillburner's **ability and endurance. 70**
miles and 7.5hrs down, 230 miles and 28.5hrs to go! #sd3

Chris Harding @The_Kraken
#sd3 **I would be dead by now, but** @hillburner **is 3/4 of**
the way through his first third of the South Downs
Way Triple. Amazing already.

June 01 at 15:25 - Simon says "Your twitter follower numbers are
going up. Now 114"

Fast

I was at one with the bike
and the iPod was thumping away.

Passing Harting I made the most of the undulations maintaining an excellent speed. Everything still continued to flow nicely and my heart rate remained low. Energy levels were good and I was still really happy. Being at one with the bike, the iPod kept thumping away, as the ground disappeared behind me.

Judy informed me at each check point how my progress was measuring up to my schedule. I had planned the ride timings meticulously on my spread sheet using information from previous South Downs rides and other calculations. It was at this point that Judy was getting excited as I was now ahead of schedule. With my heart rate low this made me feel really good.

The main information I was monitoring during the ride was the average speed and average heart rate between check points, and my overall average speed for the leg of the South Downs Way. To complete the first leg in 11 hours meant an average of 9mph. As long as I was averaging 9mph or more, I was happy. Monitoring my heart rate was crucial so I did not over exert myself and wear out too quickly.

The QECP (Queen Elizabeth Country Park) by the A3 approached quickly where Anne joined the support crew. She questioned my need for the really tatty, ripped shoes she had collected from my house. Apparently they were so muddy that she felt obliged to clean them, such dedication. They were so comfortable to wear and at this stage I wasn't fussed what they looked like.

Finishing off some more real food in the form of spaghetti bolognaise straight out of the tin, I jumped back on the bike as I needed to get to Winchester. I knew the support crew were excited and wanted to chat, but I was on a mission. Everything

was flowing nicely and I wanted to minimise the interruptions of
the check points.

83. **SevenPillarsofIgnorance**
    Actually, without a time limit, what does it mean? Fair
    play that he's going for x3; it's a big commitment, but if he
    does it in 35 hours, what does that mean, or 40, 50 hours?
    I hope he does it   but I'm not clear what "doing it means"
    is it non stop, what if he does stop, how long should he
    stop/sleep, can he get assistance, how much, etc. The
    Double, IMO, is more understandable as there is a time
    limit   so you do it, or not. Anyway, he probably, rightly,
    couldn't give a monkeys what I think, and good on him for
    giving it a go. I hope this does not sound too negative, just
    my opinion. Run the Himalayas in 100 days, unsupported?
    Madness, utter madness   but the Cranes did it, a long time
    ago.

84. **wwaswas**
    The Double, IMO, is more understandable as there is a
    time limit
    is there?

85. **portlyone**
    When he turned around will that site change his
    progress to a different colour or will loose the ability to
    track him? 😊

86. **muppetWrangler**
    The Double, IMO, is more understandable as there is a
    time limit
    Well there's not really a time limit, but I guess the
    accepted standard is 24 hours. Not that anyone's going to
    come and take your bike off you at 24:00:01.

87. **wwaswas**
    He's 11 minutes ahead of schedule after 66 miles.

88. **bugpowderdust**
    Just started raining here in Petersfield but not hard just
    enough to dampen the dust a little bit.

89. **hilldodger**
    All solo endurance challenges must seem pretty
    pointless except to the person doing them   all I can say is I
    couldn't do it, I wouldn't do it but I'd certainly doff my cap to
    anyone who tries to do it

90. **cakefest**
    *I hope he does it   but I'm not clear what "doing it
    means"   is it non stop, what if he does stop, how long
    should he stop/sleep, can he get assistance, how much,
    etc.*
    Doing it is doing it. Whatever he defines 'it' to be, and
    whatever he does. The first ascent of Everest was doing it.
    So was the ascent that someone paid $50,000 to do last
    weekend.
    Different, but still doing it.

91. **cakefest**
    Our man.
    http://i50.twitgoo.com/t66k2t.jpg

92. **wwaswas**
    Still lining his wheels up for pictures, I see 😵

93. **wwaswas**
    Smiling as much as anyone does being physio'd;

94. **Taff**
    Would like to try and ride a bit with him tomorrow. Been
    tracking him most of the day, even in my meeting.
    Awesome attempt. As if the SDWD wasn't hard enough

95. **cheese@4p**
    Good luck to the man he's set himself one hell of a
    challenge. But my money is on a DNF. Too far and its
    gonna rain.

96. **m1kea**
    There'll be another load of nutters out on the South
    Downs tomorrow as its the South Downs Relay running
    race. Sod running up and down those hills!

97. **Matt24k**

> We've been talking about doing the SDW in a day. To us that would be a real achievement. It's not a fantastic ride but it is a hell of a journey.
>
> To attempt it 3 times back to back is very impressive. My point is that it is a personal challenge and that means different things to different people. I don't see how you could knock any one for trying.

98. **owenfackrell**

> Good luck to him I say some of those hills get hard and I've only done it in a day one way (and that took 13 hours). To all those say why 3 laps? Its not 3 laps as when you turn around you are riding up the hills you came down and vis versa which makes it a very different track and by the time he's back at the beginning I doubt he will remember too much of what the ground conditions were like doing the same bits again.

the Real BeerBiker @BeerBiker
No wonder @hillburner **has a smile on his face with** @Anne24solo &@beer_babe **looking after him!** #SD3 At QE2 4 1st time!

Simon Usher @dadwithabike
#sd3 @hillburner **on fire - at QE2 ahead of schedule**

Anne Dickins @Anne24solo
Lol @hillburner **has left envelopes to keep the pit crew entertained :-) 1. Make paper aeroplanes, 2. Quiz** 3. Cool picture book to drool over

The 400 foot climb up Butser Hill is big. If you've got the energy, it's rideable, but I didn't want to waste the effort riding it a tad faster than walking pace. Getting off the bike enabled me to use alternative leg muscles. It was at this point that I was pleased that Kate had incorporated running into my training programme.

Back in training when Kate first told me to run, the fear of the cross country runs at school came to mind. I hated them and was always in the struggling group at the back. 30 years later I had to run again. Setting out for a gentle 30 minute jog I gritted my teeth. Afterwards the pains in my legs were immense. What had Kate done to me? I was supposed to do the ride of my life and my legs were shot to bits.

After a few emails to Kate and a conversation with Anne, I discovered I was suffering from DOMS (Delayed Onset Muscle Soreness) where the muscles that were not used to the exercise complain. Understanding the situation, I was happy to run again and was soon achieving 5 miles with ease.

June 01 at 16:45 - Simon says "Bike magic has tweeted your Endomondo, everyone is watching you."

Once the altitude was gained at Butser, the general trend is downhill. For a moment I thought ahead 24 hours when I would be coming into Winchester for the second time. Will I still be ecstatic to be riding my bike or would I be itching to get to the finish?

Again the speed increased as I lapped up the miles. I say miles, I wasn't actually counting the miles. I knew where I had to go, so just got on with it. If at this point I considered that I'd covered 85miles and had 215miles to go, my energy and enthusiasm would drain quickly. I enjoyed the moment and just focused on the trail 5 to 10 miles ahead of me.

Climbing the hill out from Whitewool Farm, I got to the check point at the top of the field. The lay-by was empty with no sign of the support crew. Wasting no time I pulled a marker out from my CamelBak and tied the ribbon around the gatepost, before continuing to ride. I really wasn't worried about the support crew missing the check point as we had a procedure all worked out.

In one of the planning meetings I started off by saying that the most difficult thing for the support crew was to get to the check points before me. Met with such derision that I should even contemplate the problem, I insisted that we had a procedure. Previous experience from my South Downs Double ride, had taught me the value of preparing for such an eventuality.

At some point the support crew arrived at the check point and immediately saw my marker. I've no idea what they were doing as they only had to drive a few miles whilst I was walking up Butser Hill. Flying into action they looked for an alternative check point location. There are only 2 pubs directly on the South Downs Way where Judy AKA @BeerBabe found one of them. The message came over Endomondo saying

June 01 at 17:17 - Simon says "Sorry we missed you, we are at pub if you need anything"

It was very reassuring that the simple communication method had worked, I knew exactly where the pub was so focused on getting there.

Part of the precautions taken in case there was a missed check point, was to carry enough food and drink to reach the following check point. This may sound a bit excessive, but having this reserve was deeply reassuring so I could continue on without needing more supplies.

The Milburys pub was a good land mark making an excellent check point. Feeling as though I was on a mission, which I was, I grabbed what I needed and got straight back on the trail. Winchester was neatly in sight.

June 01 at 17:18 - Simon says "You are 20 minutes ahead of schedule"

Just after the A272 crossing at Cheesefoot Head stood a lady on the bridleway. I had seen her before at Wind Farm and she wished me well again mentioning my name. I responded politely thanking her for coming to see me, but was somewhat puzzled as to who she was. My powers of recognition are not great and I should have thought a bit more about whom she could be. A Tweet later on revealed that it was Lydia Gould who was the first woman to have ridden the South Downs Double. Now if she had been wearing her Torq cycling kit, I would have recognised her instantly, as I had only met her at a few races in previous years. It was really nice of Lydia to pop up and say hello during my ride.

There was another reason for her appearance. Lydia had acted as one of the official adjudicators for the South Downs Double for the other members of the exclusive club. Along the South Downs Way are several bridleways that run next to a road. The easier route is on the smooth tarmac, but to qualify for the Double, or rather the Triple, the bridleways must be used. At Wind Farm is such place where the bridleway tucks into the trees. Lydia was obviously checking that I was not cheating. During my preparation, I made a deliberate effort to find all the places where there are such bridleways so I could follow the official route. I also included the extra 2012 addition at Eastbourne and the Temporary route via Exton introduced in 2009. This added a few more miles for me but I needed to do the full hog of the South Downs Way. If in the future someone else decides to attempt the Triple, they can't say that they did more of the route than I had done. Incidentally, if I had done the traditional pre-2009 route I would have clinched a sub-36 hour time.

To qualify for the South Downs Double ride evidence is required for the start, turnaround and finish times, along with proof of the route used. In 2009 I used a large digital clock for the timings where photos were taken of me and the clock at the specified places. I also used the GPS logs to demonstrate the route used. It's important therefore that the GPS battery does not run out. Some people have used a different GPS for each leg where I made an external battery pack containing four AAA batteries. It is then easy for someone to replace the batteries during the ride for additional longevity.

During the ride I had three clear goals that were shared with the support crew.

1. Complete the Triple
2. Achieve the Triple in less than 36 hours
3. Get a sub 23 hour Double

The purpose of the third goal was to give me something to aim for two thirds of the way along the ride. Setting intermediate targets along the way was essential to keep me on track for the big goal of the Triple. My plans were to complete each leg in 11, 12 and 13 hours, so the Double would take 23 hours. Aiming for a sub 23 hour Double would put me 3rd on the leader board for the fastest supported Double.

Rory Hitchins is another South Downs Double adjudicator. I first contacted him in September 2008 about my intention to ride the Double. At the time there were only 4 sub 24 hour Doublers who were recognised individuals established in the cycling fraternity, he was delighted that I was giving it a go. He told me that if I really wanted to conquer it, I had to do it in less than 24 hours. He later described me as someone who appeared from nowhere and nailed the Double. I was also the first person to ride the Double for a charity where supporters kindly donated over £4,000 to the BHF.

The final miles into Winchester are pretty much downhill. I stormed along the dry trails, flicked open the gates and flew down the roads.

Just after the M3 bridge was a family waiting expectantly outside their house. There was Mum & Dad with a small child between them wearing a colourful dressing gown and a younger child in their father's arms. They all stood on the pavement of Petersfield Road looking towards me. In the stillness of the street this seemed a surreal sight.

"Are you Richard?" they shouted as I approached.

"Yes" I replied in amazement as I reached them.

"Good luck – Keep going" they shouted as I disappeared down the hill.

Wow! How did they know and how nice of them to come out and see me. I assume they had been following the Endomondo tracker and realised that I would be going right past their house. This was so uplifting; I got a bit emotional when recounting the episode to the support crew. Judy kindly sent out a tweet to the family as it really was one of those special moments.

Richard Sterry @hillburner
Thanks to the family in Winchester who stood outside their gate to cheer me on my way #sd3

Winchester. I'm in Winchester. What a ride! Completing the 100 miles from Eastbourne had taken 10:08 hours, just 20 minutes off my personal best a couple of years previously. The latter half of the ride from Bury was brilliant; I had such a buzz and was looking forward to the night section on the return leg.

This is where many riders stop. The 100 miles is a tough challenge where only a couple of dozen have turned around to take on the Double. I was not even half way on my journey.

Envelope 5 - Winchester

The first leg is complete, 1 down 2 to go.

The next time we reach Winchester, celebrations will be in full swing ☺

Keep me focused, keep me going steady, so we can turn a dream into a reality.

And Back

Winchester to Eastbourne

Friday 1st June 2012 18:22

Light

*I knew exactly where I was going
and nothing was going to stop me.*

Setting off at a slightly gentler pace, I climbed out of Winchester retracing my route. I reflected on my ride so far in the comfort that I had made good time and was still feeling fresh. My legs felt great, my body was good and I felt relaxed. The sun was now losing its heat so the night time fun would soon begin.

99. **grazedknees**
    To give you all an update, Richard is on fine form. He has just done the first leg and heading back out of Winchester we are digging into the pit crew survival hamper which he left for us. He is happy and enjoying the near empty, dry trails. He is running ahead of schedule despite a puncture early on. He is riding a Scott scale 29er. Batteries have just been changed for his Endomondo.
    He says thank you for all your positive comments keep em coming!
    He had been training for months, so is as prepared as he could be. If you want a personal update we are #SD3 on twitter.

100. **avdave2**
    OK if he's made the turn we are behind on a post a mile so we need to catch up!

101. **JRTG**
    I have huge amounts of respect for someone doing this. The mental battle is a real barrier for me. Hope it all goes well and can't wait to hear all about once he finishes.

102.dobo

Fantastic challenge imo.

I wonder what he's dreading most? Not being able to eat enough and bonking? No sleep? The rain? The hills? Riding in the heat? Riding at night? Punctures?

Looks like he's coming up to Butser hill soon from the easier side, wonder if he pushes on the 3rd lap 😜

103.Taff

How is he running the Endomondo?

104.allthepies

Taff said *» How is he running the Endomondo?*

Errr, Smartphone with Endomondo app one would imagine.

105.grazedknees

He is running Endomondo off his Samsung Smartphone. Spare battery packs so hopefully it will keep live.

What's he most frightened off? The scary pit crew of course;)

106.damo2576

I don't get why he is only doing it 3 times and not 4?

107.jim76

I rode the SDW on Sunday, West to East and really enjoyed it. Never really ridden on the South Downs before and tend to be more into singletrack etc but a friend invited me along and I thought it sounded like a good challenge. It's not the most challenging riding in terms of technical sections and most of it is double track but there are some really fun sections, some super fast bits and some pretty challenging climbs. It's a real journey and certainly got me more into the idea of doing more that my usual couple of hours on the Surrey Hills.

Anyway, managed it in just over 10 hours and was pretty pleased with that. Felt pretty good on the day but on Monday and Tuesday I was exhausted! Bike was a Specialized Camber Expert Carbon with Command Post and it was superb   perfect tool for the job.

Ignore the negatives! The fact that this chap is attempting 3 times in a row gets my respect that's for sure.

4 times? Maybe he will 😬

108. **Taff**

I know it's smart phone but was wondering how it was going to keep going for 36hours. Forgot that phones had removable batteries. Been with Apple too long! 😵

South Downs is riding nicely and hope it stays like that for Richard. Will hopefully ride from the house to Winchester and back on Sunday morning. So apologies in advance for the adverse weather that day!

109. **drofluf**

Respect to the guy for doing this. I tried it one way last year and bailed after 14 hours

the Real BeerBiker @BeerBiker
1st third done, @hillburner is on his way back from Winchester to Eastbourne, leg 2 #SD3

Jo Burt @VecchioJo
@hillburner has turned round into the second 1/3rd #sdw3

Steve Girdler @stevegirdler
@hillburner South downs way - three time in 36 hrs. Amazing! You've done the training so it's all mental now. Literally. Good luck Richard

Anne Dickins @Anne24solo
@hillburner has provided a pit crew survival hamper. Yes! #Sd3
http://pic.twitter.com/YJv4wF3X

June 01 at 18:53 - Simon says "This beer is lovely"

June 01 at 18:54 - Simon says "All sorted with pub"

We agreed to meet again at the Milburys Pub where the support crew could get some proper food and I felt the need to use a decent toilet. There aren't many loos on the South Downs Way so I thought it best to make the most of this opportunity.

Our second visit to the pub in the same evening caused some interest from the locals. After explaining the nature of our mission the support crew wasted no time in collecting donations for the two charities benefiting from the ride. I had chosen the BHF, who originally got me started on the South Downs Way back in 2007, and my local church had a building project to help its work in the community. Thanks to all those who contributed as the final amount raised was nearly £1,900.

On the table outside the pub where laid out the Exposure Lights. I had contacted John Cookson from USE soon after the announcement of my Triple ride.

"Hi John, its Richard Sterry"

"Hi Richard" John replied "how are you doing?"

I could hear the penny drop as he managed to put my name into context.

We first met in 2009 where he worked with Rory who helped me with my Double ride. Our paths had crossed a few times at races and exhibitions so fortunately my name was not too unfamiliar to him.

"Doing well thanks John" I responded in an enthusiastic manner. "How are you doing?"

John gave a non-committal answer implying that he was at work and probably quite busy.

"I was wondering if you would be able to help me?" I asked gently to try to soften the blow.

"Go on…"

"I'm planning to ride the South Downs Triple"

There was silence at the end of the phone as John tried to comprehend what he heard.

"Okay" he said slowly and cautiously.

"I was wondering if USE might be able to help me with some lights?" I waited patiently for what seemed an age as John was still trying to grasp the fact that I was going to ride the South Downs Way three times. He knows others who have completed the Double and he also knows how tough it is.

"Wow, yes, of course we can. The Triple, that's a mighty long way" I could tell now that the concept of the Triple was beginning to sink in. Giving him a few moments I gabbled on about how I could return the favour with publicity on my blog site and in press releases etc.

"Which lights do you want and how many do you need? Will the support crew need some?"

His mind had now understood the enormity of the challenge and the questions kept coming.

Following the principle of 'If you don't ask, you don't get' I went for the top of the range in the form of the mighty Six-Pack an 1800 lumen monster of a light. "Oh, and I will need a Joystick for the helmet." I added. The Joystick is a small slender powerful light with a penetrating beam that can clip neatly onto the helmet.

"Yes, sure, I'll see what we can do."

This was such a relief as I hate asking for things for myself. We chatted for a few more minutes about the ride then I let John get back to his work.

Josh Ibbett, the current South Downs Double record holder who also worked at USE, kindly sent me the lights. The box arrived a few days later and it was huge, I pulled out two Six-Packs and three Joysticks. This was amazing, I was so grateful for their help.

The bright Joystick light was fitted to the helmet and the super powerful 6 Pack light found a home on the bars. It was still reasonably light but I wanted to be ready for the darkness.

The support crew somehow found time for a cheeky drink at the pub. Taking a quick sip before my departure reminded me of how good beer tasted. As part of my training regime alcohol took a back seat and in the final stages it didn't exist at all. The beer tasted particularly good and I was tempted to stay for a pint and enjoy the summer evening. This was not the reason for being on the South Downs Way so I got back on the trail.

How can you give up drinking? I was once asked. It all comes back to strong mental training and determination that Ben Hunt-Davis taught me on the motivational course. Whilst preparing for his winning Olympic row in 2000, he always asked the question "Will it make the boat go faster?" Adopting this simple decision making process, I was able to clearly focus on what would make the bike go faster. Adding an extra hill on a training ride – Yes, but a beer down the pub – probably not.

Feeling refreshed after a quick bite to eat I continued my quest. Having just ridden this section navigation was easy. In fact I didn't have to think about the route at all, it seemed so natural so most of it was completed on auto pilot. I felt as though the South Downs Way was my trail, riding alone I knew exactly where I was going and nothing was going to stop me.

Judy @beer_babe
#SD3 We now have a little convoy heading across to meet @hillburner at QECP.
All going well. Had sneaky beer at Milbury's.

Sandrita @Plum_Pudding17
@hillburner Go Richard We're in good hands with the best pit crew in UK (& the world)
with @Anne24solo @dadwithabike & @Yet2Tamer

Anne Dickins @Anne24solo
#ff Richard Sterry - @hillburner who is 1/3 into his world first south downs way triple attempt.
Go Richard!

Sheep

*There were 6 sheep standing shoulder to shoulder
across the path staring straight at me.*

I don't often ride the South Downs Way, in fact I had only
ridden each section just once during my 2012 training. It all stems
back to my preparation for the Double a few years earlier. Whilst
researching previous Double riders, and in 2008 there were not
many of them, most had made navigational errors at some point.
In a few cases it cost them a sub-24 hour time. The winter of
2008/9 was spent riding the South Downs Way in small sections
photographing every junction, and then painstakingly
documenting the whole route. This enabled me to learn and re-
live the route, committing every turn, hill, road crossing and gate
to memory. The visualisation was really powerful as I knew
exactly what was coming up next. Over the years I've got to know
some of the official names along the route. I've also made up my
own names for several other places to help me remember certain
sections.

In 2009 the new Temporary route was introduced via Exton
where the South Downs Way crosses the A32, about 10 miles
from Winchester. Personally I rather liked the traditional route via
Warnford and find the Exton alternative a bit of a pig. Heading
from Winchester; there is a long road descent to Exton and after
going through the village there is a boring flat bit on a disused
railway line. The next part weaves around some fields and has a
stupid climb up old Winchester Hill where there are steps at the
bottom. There are then bits of bridleway either side of the road
until you meet up with the traditional route.

Fortunately it was bone dry. Just 3 weeks earlier while I was
checking out the route it was completely water logged with many
unrideable sections. It was raining heavily and I got back to my car
looking like a drowned rat. Back in 2009 I took some photos of

Devil's Dyke in thick frost. I had driven an hour down the A23 and ridden in the freezing conditions. When there is a real determination to achieve a challenge, any weather can be overcome. Without such a challenge the weather can look daunting, often providing the excuse to stay inside.

The previous week of baking sun before my Triple had made such a difference to the trail conditions. Now it was so dry and fast, perfect.

Whilst weaving around the fields just beyond Exton, I came across the four guys I met at Truleigh Hill who were still wearing their colourful waterproofs. They were making good progress and would get to Winchester by nightfall. We wished each other well and I could hear them questioning my sanity as I continued on. Assuming they felt pretty knackered towards the end of one leg of the South Downs Way, they couldn't comprehend that I was doing three legs of the South Downs Way nonstop.

June 01 at 20:26 - Simon says "Tea ready! 2 sugars"

June 01 at 20:26 - Simon says "Beer biker here"

Roy (Beer Biker) had now joined the support crew; things were gearing up for the night session with Simon, Anne, Judy and now Roy. I was concerned for their safety if all of them wanted to be up all night to follow my progress. How would they be able to cope the next day when it really mattered?

Back on the main part of the South Downs Way I continued towards the QECP. Reaching Butser Hill where the official bridleway is just next to the road, I anticipated the descent. Depending on the conditions, 35-40mph is easily achievable. I wanted a grin factor but I was also aware that I needed to be sensible; a tumble at these speeds could be disastrous.

Stopping briefly at the QECP Anne reminded me to use my core muscles. She had previously coached me on waking up all the little muscles in my core to provide the stability I needed. I had frequently followed her prescriptions of exercises to gain the balance and strength required for such an endurance event. It is so easy just to focus on the big muscles, but after several hours in the saddle it can be the small stability muscles that let you down.

Anne had also masterminded the logistics for the support crew, bouncing ideas off Simon. Simulating numerous options with a map of the South Downs Way and various Lego vehicles representing myself and the members of the support crew, they hatched a plan to cover the 30 check points over the 2 days and 1 night. With the last minute change of date for the ride and then the change of direction it was amazing how Anne and Simon managed to pull everyone together. Delegating this task was a real weight off my mind during the planning and they both did particularly well as neither of them were familiar with the South Downs.

One of the things that encouraged me was how readily others were prepared to help with my crazy challenge. It takes some commitment to spend all day and all night to help someone achieve their personal goal. The quality of the support crew was of such a high calibre, I felt honoured to be amongst their company.

The sky was fairly clear with wisps of clouds that could be seen around the full moon. I deliberately chose this time for the ride because of the full moon and the double Jubilee Bank Holiday weekend. The extra holiday would ease the pressure for the support crew so they didn't need to take too much time off work. It always pays to be flexible, especially if you have to suddenly bring the event forward by two days.

Maintaining a good speed, I soon reached Harting and stopped for a pee. For some reason I always take a break at Harting, whether I need a pee or not. It's just one of those things.

Time seemed insignificant. I was aware that it was dark but the actual time was irrelevant. There was no point thinking this was my usual time for bed, as I wasn't going to bed. I was on my bike enjoying the cool night air and looking over the sleepy illuminated towns. Everything else also seemed unimportant. I was at one with my bike and nothing else appeared to matter. There were no stresses of work or life, there was just me enjoying the moment as the ground rushed past below me.

June 01 at 22:19 - Simon says "Hot cup of tea waiting for you at Cocking"

June 01 at 22:20 - Simon says "Remember Nellie the elephant packed her trunk"

The descent to Cocking was fast. Flicking the lights up to full power, it was like riding in daylight and my speed was not compromised. This time the support crew were at the car park where they refuelled me for the next section.

Richard Sterry @hillburner
#sd3 Special thanks to @dadwithabike & @Anne24solo for filling my head with 'Nellie the Elephant'! I need my iPod!!

110.**grazedknees**
       Update: it's now properly dark but we can see Richard on the horizon with his six pack dropping into Cocking. His iPod has broken so he will be humming his favourite tunes through the night. He is still cheerful and enjoying hearing the comments from singletrack massive.

111.**richen987**
       Been keeping a watch on this, really impressive, incredible to keep
       an average at over 9mph for so long. Good luck and will check in the morning.

112.jameso

> I hope he's humming better tunes than the ones that come into my head when I'm on a long (for me) ride. Really awful, some of them.
>
> Best of luck for a good night's riding to him. Look fwd to hearing that he did it, sometime tomorrow!

113.Taff

> Is he in the pub? Been still around Amberley for a while

114.splashdown

> Good luck 😎

Anne Dickins @Anne24solo
Another scorching CP for @hillburner - you can see where he has been by the flames in the trail. #sd3

The Exposure lights were brilliant. The Joystick light was brighter than previous versions and the 6 Pack light was brighter than the full moon. On the chalky sections I had to turn the brightness down to prevent it dazzling my eyes.

The wheels were still turning and the miles were clocking up nicely. I felt good. I love night riding, especially cross country solo night riding. It's like entering a new world shared with the wildlife as the deer, badgers and owls allow you to enter their kingdom. There are also the sheep. I am fully aware of sheep at night time.

Riding the Double in 2009, I passed through the field at Glatting Beacon around 11pm. Entering at the corner of the field, the bridleway goes along the perimeter fence. Most of the sheep, the ones with the brain cells, retreated into the centre of the field; however some were not so intelligent. They followed the bridleway in the direction I was heading. Riding at about 15mph, the sheep were running flat out trying to keep head of me. All they had to do was to go into the centre of the field, but they continued forward. Puzzled by their stupidity, what happened next was a complete surprise. The 6 or 8 sheep suddenly turned and charged towards me. I let out a mighty ROAR, and then we collided. I was hit from all directions with one sheep head butting me quite painfully in the buttock. How I stayed on the bike, I don't know, somehow I remained upright, I stood on the pedals and raced to the end of the field. As for the sheep, I don't think they suffered much damage, except for their pride.

Entering this same field for my Triple, again around 11pm, I approached it cautiously. Looking ahead, there were 6 sheep standing shoulder to shoulder across the path staring straight at me. They glared with their glowing eyes from the reflection of my lights. Riding with determination towards them, they stood firm defending their field. My loud hissing penetrated the air until all their self-confidence evaporated, making them scarper into the centre of the field. Conflict over.

Dark

Drink drink drink

Meeting the support crew at Bury, they were all togged up in warmer clothes and kitted out with lights in and around the van. I had already added an extra top and some leggings back at the Milburys pub, so felt comfortable with the dropping temperature.

During the refuelling at Bury, a couple of lights were twinkling further down the track. On my descent I met Rory Hitchins and Frazer Clifford who had postponed their bedtime to ride with me. Delighted to have some company, we made it to the bottom of the hill and crossed over the river Arun. Rory has been noted for describing the Double as;

"It's not about the ride there, it's about the ride back."

Reaching the foot of Amberley Rise Rory had to bow out due to a persistent puncture. We wished each other well as Frazer and I headed up the hill. Amberley Rise is a steep climb that marks the halfway point of the South Downs Way and for me the halfway point of the Triple. These aspects never entered my head as I was just enjoying the moment.

Once on the ridge we made good progress. Our lights illuminated the trail and we could see the glow from the towns below. Another light could be seen in the distance, which turned out to be JP Saville from Quest Adventure, who had come out to find me. News was spreading fast and he wanted to see part of the action.

With strong legs, the A24 soon appeared for another brief check point before I climbed up to Chanctonbury Rings. I think I rode this alone so I guess Frazer and JP had departed.

Saturday at 00:29 - Simon says "Dan says come on son Dan says come on son"

My son Dan was obviously still up and I appreciated his comment sent via the support crew. Time for bed Dan.

The air was quiet and so was my iPod, the battery had finally given out. The only sound was the noise of the tyres rolling effortlessly along the trail. In the valleys below were the silent towns sleeping with little knowledge that a piece of history was in the making.

I don't mind riding in silence as it gives me time to think or to sometimes to listen. The gentle rumblings of the tyres told me I was travelling at a good speed. Focusing on the sound for several minutes causes the rest of my thoughts to evaporate. As my mind rests and it's incredibly peaceful. I think they call this 'being in the zone' where nothing else matters. I can ride in this state for tens of minutes where the time just flies by. An interruption would flick me out of the daze bringing me back to full consciousness. During my winter training I often spent an hour or two on the turbo trainer, sometimes without any music so I could practice getting into the zone. A whole evening would disappear in what seemed just a few minutes.

I spent a few moments thinking about what I was doing; riding alone on the tops of the hills in the dark and in the middle of the night. Out of context this sounds crazy but I wasn't scared about being on my own, I was relaxed and enjoying the tranquillity of the silence and the stillness all around me. It was a wonderful feeling.

Envelope 7 - Washington

As night draws in, I don't want you getting bored.

Here are some CDs to help the time pass.

Think about some appropriate and inappropriate song choices for a play list.

115.grazedknees

Richard is in really good spirits he is riding consistently and fuelling well. No real aches or pains although he hit his shoulder against a gate so is a bit sore.

He has given the pit crew surprise envelopes at certain check points, this one is a compilation of cheesy 80s tunes. Roll on a night with Bananarama, Genesis and Wham! Cue the next pit stop having the speakers on full volume. I hope the sheep appreciate it.

frazer clifford @frazer72
Just back from a ride
with @retrorory **chasing** @hillburner **! Haha. That's not a normal time to be creeping in for a shower.**

frazer clifford @frazer72
@hillburner **looked very strong at 1am. Keep it up Richard.**

Taking each bit at a time the climb up Beeding Hill to the Youth Hostel wasn't too bad. Three years previously when I was riding the Double, I ran out of energy at this point and struggled to keep going in the heat. Friend Alex Bottomley made a surprise visit to join me on the Double and realised I was suffering from dehydration. Alex, an experienced rider, coaxed me to the tap at the Youth Hostel to cool down and get back some fluids.

This time I wasn't suffering from overheating, but I was feeling a bit sick. My mouth was dry and I wanted to drink but I was finding the High5 drink unpalatable. In any endurance event it can be difficult to predict exactly what you want to eat as your palate changes and strange cravings can occur. Eventually making the connection, it was the sweetness of the High5 that upset me whereas the Torq energy drink was OK.

A decision was made to switch and stay on the Torq drink, however this caused a problem. I had only planned to use the Torq drink for a part of the ride so only packed one small tub of the powder. The support crew calculated that it would run out at

9am. Where do you get a tub of Torq drink at 1am in the morning? Oh, and I'm fussy on my flavours, I only like the Torq Vanilla.

Saturday at 02:01 - Simon says "Boys are asleep but girls ready to party"

Saturday at 02:10 - Simon says "Keep those feet turning"

The undulating climb up to Devils Dyke can be challenging, but in the darkness and wrapped up in my thoughts the final gate appeared quickly. Crossing the field and the road, I descended to the check point at Saddlescombe.

It was still dark and the support crew warned me about a group of people who were walking a section of the South Downs Way by night. An interesting challenge, that's about as insane as riding the South Downs Way by night.

The group of walkers were armed with hiking sticks and head torches, preceded quietly in single file in the darkness. Passing them near Pyecombe golf course, I continued up the hill towards Ditchling Beacon.

I had to focus, the iPod was dead and the spare wasn't working so all I had was the sound of my own voice to disturb the wildlife. My mind kept fading in the darkness and I would suddenly pull it back to reality. A mixture of supportive and mad comments came over the Endomondo from the support crew to amuse me.

Saturday at 02:49 - Simon says "Drink drink drink"

Saturday at 02:51 - Simon says "Have a gel please"

Saturday at 02:54 - Simon says "Drink drink drink"

Saturday at 02:55 - Simon says "Did you have a gell?"

Saturday at 02:59 - Simon says "Cup of tea is waiting for you!"

Saturday at 03:00 - Simon says "But you can't have it until you have had a gel"

"Yes I've had a drink!"

"And a gel!"

My shouts were pointless as they couldn't hear me but they released some aggression as I climbed up to Ditchling Beacon.

Saturday at 03:06 - Simon says "Hurray over the big hill"

Saturday at 03:07 - Simon says "Go Hill Burner burn those hills"

Saturday at 03:08 - Simon says "Just opening envelope 9"

Saturday at 03:09 - Simon says "It feels interesting"

Saturday at 03:09 - Simon says "We are laughing. Brilliant. Flashing pens"

Saturday at 03:12 - Simon says "We are flashing"

Saturday at 03:12 - Simon says "Thank you Richard"

Saturday at 03:12 - Simon says "We are having so much fun"

Saturday at 03:13 - Simon says "Are you over that hill yet"

Saturday at 03:18 - Simon says "Almost there. Think about your hot cup of tea"

Saturday at 03:19 - Simon says "Lots more twitter follower for you"

Saturday at 03:22 - Simon says "Have you overtaken the walkers?"

Saturday at 03:30 - Simon says "Drink drink drink"

Saturday at 03:31 - Simon says "Think about everything which feels good"

Saturday at 03:35 - Simon says "Pedal pedal pedal"

Saturday at 03:40 - Simon says "We want to see your smiling face"

Saturday at 04:13 - Simon says "Simon message from Simon message to Simon. Confusion"

Anne & Judy used the Endomondo pep talks to the full, it kept them awake provided me with some entertainment. Without an iPod any sort of company was appreciated during the most difficult hours of the night.

Stopping briefly at the A27 I really didn't feel like eating anything. My stomach felt fragile, I still felt a bit sick and I didn't fancy drinking. Anne in her wisdom had prepared a warm and soft ginger energy bar. It slipped down nicely where the ginger is good for settling the stomach. It is this attention to detail that the experience of the support crew really showed.

Just Judy and Anne were in the Black Pig this time as Simon and Roy were left at the last check point to get some rest. Unfortunately in the girls excitement waiting for my arrival, the van lights were left on. Consequently when trying to depart, the battery was flat. Waking the boys up they had to wait for a jump start before proceeding to the next check point. This extra drama and reduced sleep added to their tiredness in the darkness of the night.

116.grazedknees

4.03 am. Richard has just been through the A27 checkpoint. The last leg was a bit slower due to a heavy mist that has fallen making navigating tricky. It's still dry and warm and the trails dusty. He isn't complaining of any body problems although he is not enjoying eating, who would at 4am?! He is still joking with us and really looking forward to the dawn arriving. Still 10 minutes ahead of schedule.

117.Angus Wells

Watching progress from here in Jordan. So here is an early morning cheer to keep the morale up. Hurrah.

Dawn

Buttercups

The next few miles were ridden in silence. It was an eerie silence that suddenly became very loud. No, it wasn't my imagination, but the dawn chorus had started. If you've ever been up all night, the dawn chorus can appear deafening. What surprised me was that there were no trees nearby where I assumed the birds lived. The sound of the birds singing is the first sign of morning. The second sign is seeing the silhouettes of the trees. There is usually an air of anticipation as the landscape is slowly revealed. In the sky appears a majestic deep rich blue colour that gradually lightens as the daylight starts to take hold.

If you are lucky enough to experience the most spectacular part, the sun rising can be fantastic. The warm glow that floods the sky provides a complete sense of forgiveness from all the pain experienced during the night. A new day has dawned.

Today, I missed the sunrise due to the cloud, but I was happy that we were into a new day.

Climbing the long assent after the A26 I became aware of the low cloud or fog. Reaching the top by the radio masts, the fog became very thick reducing visibility down to just 20 metres. This isn't too bad where the trail is well defined, but in the open areas it's a matter of aiming for the distant gate or marker post, a slight wander off the trail can be disastrous.

Flicking the Exposure 6 Pack onto maximum extended the visibility to a valuable 50 metres. Concentrating hard on the trail, I noticed the yellow buttercups only grew in the slightly longer grass on the edge of the trail.

"Stay away from the buttercups" I kept reminding myself. I had to keep reminding myself as my memory was weak. Clocking up 22 hours on the bike was taking its toll.

During the last minute panic when we brought the start of the ride forward by two days, I had forgotten to load the South Downs Way route into my GPS. Resorting to memory and keeping away from the buttercups I pushed on.

Gathering around the gate at Firle car park was a herd of supporters. I say 'herd' as the cows completely surrounded the gate blocking my route. Judy stepped into action to refine her cow talking technique. They are not the fastest moving animals around, but somehow she persuaded them to clear a way for me to get past. Meanwhile Anne gave me appropriate warnings via Endomondo so I arrived prepared to see the extra welcomers.

Saturday at 04:36 - Simon says "Lots of cows in misty fields beware"

Saturday at 04:36 - Simon says "Dawn is here hurrah"

Saturday at 04:39 - Simon says "Drink drink"

Saturday at 04:39 - Simon says "Watch for cows just before checkpoint"

Simon Usher @dadwithabike
@hillburner: **Now to navigate past a massive heard of curious cows who have blocked the gate. Wearing red wasn't so clever eh?** #sd3

When the support crew topped up my supplies they realised I was not eating or drinking much. They encouraged me to eat but this was the last thing I wanted. Concerns were rising about my diminishing condition where completing just the Double was in question. Fortunately they kept their thoughts to themselves and supplied me with plenty of encouragement.

Soon after Firle Beacon there is a very subtle fork to the left, with the main trail veering slightly to the right. The fog was still very evident making navigation crucial. Staying away from the buttercups would keep me on the trail, but I needed to remain on the South Downs Way. On a recce ride, I noticed the white chalk turns briefly brown just before the fork. Crossing over to the left of the trail at the brown chalk, I found myself approaching the correct gate for the next field. This was quite a relief as I had no technology to rely on and thinking about getting back on the track would be difficult and time consuming.

On the descent to Alfriston I stopped for a pee. There would not be many other opportunities before Eastbourne, or until this point on the way back. My stomach was still all over the place and I was now feeling sick. I tried to retch hoping that something would come out. I tried again, nothing happened. Frustrated and conscious of time, I pushed on. In fact I'd been pushing on for the past few miles. My goal for a sub 23 hour Double was getting tight. I knew how many miles and hills there were to Eastbourne and time was slipping away.

I could tell my body was weakening, random thoughts circulated in my head with no conclusions, I felt tired, my stomach wasn't right and I could feel the energy draining out of my body. Surprisingly my legs were OK, they just kept on going without complaining. I wanted that sub 23 hour Double so I made sure that I got it.

118.**FunkyDunc**
Has he stopped? Endomondo is no longer saying live, or at least it isn't to me?

119.**spooky_b329**
Says live for me, and it's refreshing as it does that annoying 'zoom out' whilst you are hunting for his position. He is on the climb out of Alfriston.

120.**grazedknees**
He is still going, heading to Eastbourne. He was feeling a bit sick on the last checkpoint and hips are a bit sore. A bit of a struggle to get through a herd of cows. He was keen to know who was following his progress and says thank you for all the encouragement.

121.FunkyDunc

Now showing live on mine again.

The quickest and easiest way to find out where he is, is to hover over the graph at the bottom at the far right hand side of the graph, it then puts a red dot on the map which is where he is.

122.oldgit

That's a hearty ride, hats off to him. My head couldn't do that even if my legs could.

Richard Sterry @hillburner
Long climb out of Alfriston and legs are feeling it.
Thinking of my mum who has probably also had a sleepless night. Thanks mum:-)

Anne Dickins @Anne24solo
@hillburner is almost at the double. Most people would put their going home legs on- but he will have another 100 miles to do.... #sd3

the Real BeerBiker @BeerBiker
Thick fog above Jevington as @hillburner heads for the turnaround at Eastbourne #SD3 come & join us for leg 3 all welcome

Jon Linscott @jonlinscott
@hillburner - keep going Richard. you're doing great!

Seeing afterwards this tweet from friend Jon Linscott, his timing was perfect. Jon was on my support crew when I rode the Double and it was at this point approaching Eastbourne that he rode with me. On the Double I really struggled to climb these massive hills so Jon in his gentle humorous way coaxed me up the long inclines.

Anne and Judy were back on the Endomondo.

Saturday at 06:11 - Simon says "T shirts have arrived!"

Saturday at 06:11 - Simon says "They look fantastic."

Saturday at 06:11 - Simon says "Hurry to Eastbourne to see our new T shirts."

Saturday at 06:12 - Simon says "You will be so proud to wear it so keep going."

Saturday at 06:26 - Simon says "We have located some Vanilla drink too."

Saturday at 06:26 - Simon says "The world is all helping you."

Saturday at 06:27 - Simon says "Hip Hip hooray"

Climbing the long chalky hill out of Jevington was tough, my determination kicked in and the pedals kept moving. After the golf course I consciously had to bear right to reach the new Eastbourne end of the South Downs Way. Knowing that Paradise Drive was just off to my left, where the South Downs Way used to finish, the extension of the South Downs Way seemed to continue on for miles as the minutes ticked by.

All tiredness disappeared as I rounded the corner to the final descent. Full of excitement I reached the final South Downs Way marker with shouts of joy from the support crew.

22:55 hours for the South Downs Double, 36 minutes faster than my Double in 2009, what an achievement. Everyone was delighted that goal No.3 was in the bag.

Sean Skinner @SeanUSX
Amazing to see @hillburner has done the South Downs Double 200 miles in 22:55 and is now doing a further 100 miles! Keep going!#SD3

Envelope 10 - Eastbourne

The South Downs Double is complete – Yay!

Hopefully, we've made it in 23 hours.

Now the challenge really begins, give me things to look forward to at the next check point. Perhaps something special to eat or drink, someone to meet, the answer to a joke (you may have to repeat the question if I forget it), or something else.

Remember to get some rest and let's enjoy making history.

And There Again

Eastbourne to Winchester

Saturday 2nd June 2012 06:59

Dr Jerry

Dr Jerry powered up in his 4x4
and set to work.

Dr Jerry Hill had driven down to Eastbourne and immediately stepped into action. He is an expert in trauma medicine and emergency care. In the sporting arena he has worked with jockeys, footballers, the Royal Ballet and the England Tap Team. More recently he was a Games Maker for the Olympics and Paralympics. Dr Jerry met Anne at one of the numerous test events for 2012 in the Velodrome, when she asked him to join the support crew he thought it sounded like fun. Little did he know what was in store for him.

Thrusting a thermometer in my mouth and fitting a device on my wrist to measure my blood pressure, he noted the results. This became a pattern at every subsequent check point although he never told me the figures. I therefore had no idea how my body was fairing. On reflection, if he had given me the numbers, they wouldn't have meant anything and would only have clogged up my weakening brain with the extra information.

Dr Jerry had a crucial role to play to ensure I got home alive. He was thorough in his tests and assessments, coupled with a very good bike side manner. Although he was not that familiar with cycling, he was a real team player rolling up his sleeves to get stuck in with anything that was required.

The South Downs Double was a major accomplishment with 200 miles behind me. This is where the previous two dozen Doublers had stopped. To ride the Triple was going to be something else, no one had ever tried it before and I was going to make history. All the extra preparation was for this third leg and the risks were high.

123.**grazedknees**

Yeee haa! Richard managed to get to Eastbourne in 22.55. I believe that puts him on the leader board. Big smiles. He passed the Dr test, and with a huge whoop and a smile the size of the Solent he has turned round and gone over the brow of the hill. Go Richard!!!!

124.**offthebrakes**

Great stuff!

Anne, have you managed to infiltrate his brain with more terrible music?

125.**superfli**

Fk me, it seems like ages since I started watching his progress! A day at work, eve, a sleep, and he's still going, and will be until this eve 😳

HUGE RESPECT!

126.**JRTG**

He's doing amazingly well. Great pace, heading up on the hills soon, will look out for him!

127.**wisepranker**

The man's quite clearly insane!

128.**nsaints**

HUGE RESPECT!

+1

Keep going Richard, you can do it

I'm keeping a close eye on progress whilst running a huge update of contracts into SAP. I've just rewritten my script so it's running faster...Richards still going to cross the finish line ahead of me

129.**cakefest**

Stunning effort, Richard. Savour every little bit. This is living.

130.**MarkSS**

Awesome stuff.

"Because its there"   that's the spirit.

131.Cheezpleez
  Seriously impressive! Go on mate, keep those pedals
  turning!

132.Taff
  Glad to hear he's got through the night ok.

the Real BeerBiker @BeerBiker
Yeah Eastbourne end of 2nd leg 22h55m on the new
course for @hillburner a record? Leg 3 underway.
Winchester here we come again #SD3

Antony Gray @antonygray
@hillburner nice one Richard keep it going !!

jimbosussexmtb @jimbosussexmtb
@hillburner God on him, keep it going :-) #Sd3

jimbosussexmtb @jimbosussexmtb
@hillburner or even "good on him" which was what I
meant! #damnautocorrect #Sd3

Jimbosussexmtb was right the first time, without an iPod I
focused my thoughts on others – praying for their situations
whilst being grateful for the fantastic journey I was travelling.

Simon was the first rider to be my safety companion. I know
this is a solo ride but it just wasn't safe for me to be alone out on
the hills at this stage. Our rules were strict; the safety rider had to
let me lead the way, set the pace, open the gates and ride as if I
was riding solo.

We climbed slowly and painfully out of Eastbourne. Every
pedal turn was an effort, my body felt awful. Firle seemed a

million miles away and I was struggling with the gentle climb across the golf course. Calling to Simon, I told him I needed the support crew before Firle. I didn't know what I wanted but I knew I needed help. He made a call as I descended to Jevington.

Finding a bench by the road I propped up the bike and lay down. This was the first time I had been horizontal for 24 hours. All the elation of completing the Double was gone, which was replaced by exhaustion and sickness.

Dr Jerry powered up in his 4x4 and set to work. Giving me something for my sickness I think he also said something that gave me the encouragement to keep going. Simon and I mounted our bikes to continue to Alfriston. The hills seemed vast.

Luke Burstow @LukeBurstow
@hillburner **absolutely fantastic ride. Somewhat lost for words, tbh. Chapeaux.** #SD3

James Brickell @WolvoBricks
@hillburner **is passing our house soon. Go on fella, 3 times SDW is gonna hurt!**

Steve Golding @stevegolding2
@hillburner **Amazing effort Richard. Met you at Firle. What an inspiration to us all! Keep going, reach that finish line & set a new record!**

John McFaul @JohnMcFaul
@hillburner **This is the bit that counts Rich.** #sd3

Saturday at 08:06 - Simon says "You're going great. Each pedal stroke gets you closer to Winchester"

Descending to Alfriston, the support crew made an impromptu appearance. I think some food or drink was administered before I set off. Judy and Roy, who met when they were rally driver navigators, knew the South Downs really well. This added an essential ingredient to the support crew so they could quickly catch me up on the trails.

I was now very much in the hands of the support crew as my body was rapidly weakening. They were making more of the decisions on my behalf to try to keep me on the bike. Latterly I discovered that many times they had serious doubts if I would even make it to the next check point. This extra check point was one of those moments.

Climbing up to Firle was a long hard slog and Simon with his fresh legs patiently let me set the pace. Simon has a great sense of perspective and a tactful ability to guide decisions. He provides stability and calmness to any fraught situation and made an excellent support manger. It was his foresight and poignant text the previous day that made us bring the event forward by two days. In hindsight, if we had not advanced the date, there wouldn't have been another appropriate weather window for at least a couple of months.

133. Napalm

It looks to me that the Endomondo graph is not recording his current progress and that Richard's still in Eastbourne.

Can anyone confirm that he's still moving and what time he might hit Firle Beacon?

134. offthebrakes

His schedule for Firle Beacon is shortly after 8am. Looks like he is maybe 15 20 mins ahead of schedule at Eastbourne.

Latest tweets confirmed he'd left Eastbourne, I think Endomondo updates in chunks rather than continuously, so I doubt he's stopped.

135. **muddy@rseguy**

Well it looks like he's either started or is just about to start the return leg from Eastbourne...good going 😃

(bit difficult to get the map update thingy to work)

Bet he's going to enjoy the long downhill into Southease today 😎

136. **Napalm**

Ok, the graph has updated.

I do find hitting F5 very refreshing.

137. **singletrackmind**

So he is, I think, the third fastest 'Double Supported' rider after Mike Cotty and Neil Newell. After holding back on the gas and keeping a reserve for another 100 mile ride!

Is Richard a machine? Is he actually on a Puch maxi 50? Can anyone confirm he is not on a tandem with Jan Ulrich as stoker?

Clearly super fit and super fast. Riding one way in a paltry 13 hrs left me pretty much destroyed so I don't know how you mentally prepare for the pain this must put you through

.

You can tell from the earlier posts who has ridden a lot of the SDW and who hasn't.

Is anyone heading up on to the Downs (who is fast enough to keep up) to give him a load of encouragement / stop him nodding off?

The London Bike Show @londonbikeshow
Follow @hillburner he's riding the SouthdownsWay x3 for fun!! Well over 300 non-stop. Rode with him for a burst last night #strong

Steve Golding @stevegolding2
@hillburner Rich. This is the most amazing thing I've seen in years. You can do this.

Kate Potter @KPOTTERxo
@hillburner Thinking of you Rich, no need to rush, 1
pedal stroke at a time, stay in zone & count down
those miles as you leave them behind.

jim russell @jimification
@hillburner Hey, It's Jim with the Cannondale - Was
nice to ride with you yesterday. Keep turning the
pedals and keep the rubber side down!

Jo Burt @VecchioJo
I've ridden to say hello, ridden a bit more, got home
and had a bath, @hillburner is still going #forza

Morgan Pilley @MorgoPilley
@BeerBiker @hillburner That's a solid ride....respect.

Supporters

*Beware of strange men
presenting gifts*

Back in Jevington we had passed a large group of runners who were doing a relay event on the South Downs Way. Spread out across the hills we slowly caught them up on the descents, where they beat us on the climbs. I must have been going really slowly to be overtaken by a runner. This cat and mouse process felt somewhat embarrassing, but they were fresh and I had been riding all night.

My legs found their form and kept the wheels turning. I remember my stomach was feeling a bit better at Firle as I introduced Simon to the late braking game on the descent to the A26.

138. **offthebrakes**
And now it's updated, he's climbing out of Jevington.

139. **Napalm**
OK heading off shortly to meet him somewhere around Itford Hill.

140. **offthebrakes**
Good luck Simon. I am meeting him at Bury, if you're still there I'll see you too. Seriously worried that he'll be too fast for me even after 250 miles!

141. **njee20**
So he is, I think, the third fastest 'Double   Supported' rider after Mike Cotty and Neil Newell. After holding back on the gas and keeping a reserve for another 100 mile ride!

Not detracting in any way, because it's a storming effort, but that's more because folk focused on doing it unsupported!

142.**wwaswas**

Fantastic ride. I just can't imagine having the stamina to do this

143.**splashdown**

Sorry if this has already been posted...

More information available here http://www.sterry.org/

In addition to an amazing effort he's also hoping to raise funds for a couple of charities

Donated 😃

144.**iomnigel**

Go on lad! Amazing feat of endurance stamina and mental strength. When will the first 36hr MTB race start??

145.**richen987**

Woke up and he is on third leg! Cracking effort keep pushing!

146.**ir_bandito**

Good effort. Makes my Trans Cambrian Way ITT tomorrow pale into insignificance...

And, am I the only one who sniggered at this:

his six pack dropping into Cocking

[See comment No. 110]

147.**Napalm**

I'm at Itford Hill, lots of off road relay runners & no cyclists. Has he gone past already?

148.**JoB**

He should be right with you Napalm

149.**Kojaklollipop**
Saw him about 30mins ago around Bo Peep, still looking strong. Amazing effort!

150.**spooky_b329**
Now shows him on the swing bridge at Southease, so if you ain't seen him yet Napalm, I think you've missed him!

151.**Napalm**
He shot past with one support rider; now waiting outside Kiri Te Kanawa's house to see him again & maybe follow. By eck they look fast & fresh.

152.**Ming the Merciless**
Top banana! Took me 14hrs 35 just to do it one way and I was broken for a month afterwards.

153.**Napalm**
Lots of walkers   Duke of Edinburgh event   here they come now.

154.**Napalm**
2 weary cyclists just gone past; but it wasn't Richard, here he comes =1 now. Soon to hit yellow brick road.

Climbing the awkward hill at Rodmell was a cyclist taking a photo of us. This was Simon Catmur who asked me if it was OK for him to put the picture on the Singletrack World forum. Somewhat puzzled by the request, I agreed and enquired a bit further. Apparently a thread on the forum about my ride was into its fifth page of comments, so he wanted to add a live picture. There seemed to be a bit of a social buzz about my adventure and I wasn't quite sure what to make of it.

There were now two riders following me, which soon became one when Simon Usher punctured. We had agreed in advance that I would not stop to help. It sounds a bit selfish, but I had a ride to complete and the clock was ticking.

155.Napalm
Support rider has front flat, I'm waiting for him (Simon) as he'll get lost here. Richard about to drop to support car on A27 bridge.

The descent to the A27 was a bit awkward with the runners spaced about 50 metres apart. Timing my arrival to the narrow section carefully I didn't want to clash with the others and put myself under too much pressure.

Envelope 11 – A27

The challenge is on, but don't forget about yourself. Freshen yourself up and grab a nice coffee or breakfast to keep you going.

Here are some flags to add some colour to the day.

The A27 by Housedean Farm was also a changeover point for the relay event so the lay-by was rather crowded. My support crew were easy to spot as the Black Pig was decked out with bright Union Jacks and each person was wearing matching blue printed T shirts describing my ride. It almost looked professional. Custom T shirts worked well for my Double ride so we improved the quality for the Triple. Due to the earlier start date, we had to get them delivered directly to the South Downs Way start at Eastbourne. For some reason the delivery driver left them at the nearby school so the support crew arranged for the school to leave them in a yellow roadside grit container overnight. These creative logistics worked enabling the support crew to wear the T shirts for the final leg of the Triple.

The support crew were pleased to see that I looked a little better although a bit puzzled that I had dropped Simon Usher.

Whilst taking on some solid food I enquired about a bystander who had also been at the last few check points with a rather large camera. Introduced to Mike Anton who was following my progress I was moved by all the attention I was attracting. Mike kindly withheld his camera during a crucial Chamois moment. (The need to apply cream to prevent saddle sores)

Anne noticed my hands were suffering with the constant pressure on the handlebars so inserted extra padding into my gloves. A second pair of shorts was provided to give extra padding for my bum.

Leaving the A27 Judy said "Beware of strange men presenting gifts." Rather puzzled by her comment, I parked the thought and rode on. Simon Catmur soon caught up with me again as we climbed to the ridge at Plumpton Plain. The heat of the sun was behind us as we made good progress overtaking the runners.

As my stomach started to settle down my speed picked up. I can't remember what I was thinking about because my brain was not really with it. The pain and exhaustion was very real but I couldn't feel it. I was so focused on my goal that nothing else mattered.

This is what's called going through the pain barrier. Everything hurt so much that I could no longer feel it. It provided a false sense of security that has to be very carefully monitored by the support crew.

Approaching Ditchling Beacon we skirted around the busy car park to find Roy holding out his hand. Taking the gift whilst still riding, I licked and sucked the refreshingly cool ice cream without dropping it. I wasn't sure how the sweetness would fair with my delicate stomach, so I focused on my appreciation of Roy's thoughtfulness and left my stomach to sort itself out.

Roy added an extra quality to the support crew. He left the others to do the regular bits for my nutrition and medical needs and focused on the finishing touches. Bombing around on the roads, he popped up in all manner of places on the South Downs Way, providing morale support and boosting my motivation. He was also able to report back to the support crew on my current condition so they could prepare for the next check point.

Saturday at 11:21 - Simon says "Go Richard go Richard go Richard we are all routing for you"

Reaching Saddlescombe, there was another large crowd and they weren't all there for the runners. The supporters for the runners were by now fully aware of my quest and joined in to encourage me.

Anne asked her regular question when I arrived.

"Tell me what hurts"

I thought about my body to try to identify what was hurting the most. A new pain had started in my left leg.

"My left knee" I responded.

"You're going to have to drop your trousers." She said in her official physiotherapist voice.

In the middle of the car park my outer shorts and leggings were slid down leaving my original shorts for privacy. I was beyond caring at this point she could have asked me to do anything.

"Unfortunately it's going to be pink." Anne explained.

I had no idea what she was talking about until she produced her pink strapping tape and applied it around my knee.

I saw a group of cyclists to my left. "They are your supporters" I was informed. They kept a slight distance from the support crew so not to get in the way. One was Josh Ibbett whom I'd not yet met and had kindly brought along a tub of Torq energy drink in Vanilla. He was given the tub for completing his record breaking South Downs Double in 17:47 hours and was prepared to give it to me. There's a huge mountain biking following in the Brighton area and various communications in the early hours of the morning managed to locate the much needed Torq drink.

"Can you ask Josh to come over"

Josh came over and we were introduced; I thanked him for sending the Exposure lights and for his support.

156.jet26

Impressive   very impressive!

157.Matt24k

Is it just me or is the Endomondo thing really that frustrating to use. Every time I zoom in to try and get a fix on our man it zooms back out again. That aside what a fantastic effort and I hope the weather and walkers stay kind.

158.spooky_b329

I moaned about this earlier, the tip given was to hover the mouse over the route profile and it will highlight on the map. So move to the end of the profile and it will show his position.

159.cakefest

Can't see route profile in Endomondo to find where he is. Do I need to create a login or something?

160.tenfoot

Massive respect to this man. Fantastic effort.

161.StefMcDef

Chapeau for this chap. More power to his pedals. A superhuman feat.

162.Matt24k

Here's the Endomondo link that was given about 4 pages back on the thread so could do with re posting: http://www.endomondo.com/workouts/60289217 As mentioned above by spooky_b329 if you hover your cursor of the end of the profile graph a red dot shows on the map for his current position. It looks like he has 70 miles to go.

163.**faz083**

    235 miles in 28 hours. That's amazing.

164.**m1kea**

    I popped out to get some snaps
    Richard & Josh Ibbett at the Saddlescombe pitstop
Apparently Josh has done a ride or two himself? 😊

165.**m1kea**

    When I left them at 11:30 he was still averaging
7.7mph. Some other guys joined him at that point and I
hope others will get out there as well.

    Plus, put your hands in your pockets and donate a bit.

166.**cinnamon_girl**

    Blimey 😳

    Go that man! Brilliant stuff.

167.**Matt24k**

    Link to Just Giving page
http://www.justgiving.com/teams/southdownstriple
I don't know Richard but I am inspired by this ride.

168.**smiff**

    That's awesome. Good support team essential. He runs
a lot of sag in his forks. hardtail so his arse must be taking
a pounding...

169.**m1kea**

    *That's awesome. Good support team essential. He runs
a lot of sag in his forks. hardtail so his arse must be taking
a pounding...*

    He had an 'Assos creme' moment at Housdean but I
didn't snap that! 😄

    His support are also pretty tired and speaking with other
long distance / duration competitors, it's vital to have a
good crew and that they stay fresh as well.

    Gee them up to if you get out to watch the final 6 hours
or so.

170.**zippykona**
> I can't even ride to work on a hardtail.
> Super bloody human. Man of the year etc.

Setting off up to Devils Dyke the group of cyclists followed me. Climbing up the hill I heard my name being called from someone running towards me. "Richard" "Richard" It was Mark Raffield from Redhill Cycling Club. Mark is an inspiration to anyone who has been seriously injured. A few years ago he received a near death experience having come off his bike. He got the paramedics very worried as he was being rushed to hospital, and then spent several days in intensive care. Making a full recovery a year later Mark rode further than he had ever ridden before and completed the BHF Randonnée, 100 miles of the South Downs Way. Repeating the Randonnée several times in subsequent years, he showed such determination and courage to overcome his accident. Well done Mark.

Mark had made a special effort to come and see me, which meant so much. We shared a few warm words as he ran and I pedalled slowly up the hill.

Unable to make much more conversation, Simon Usher who had caught up with us made the introductions with those riding behind me. John Lemonius, Gavin Thomson and Jo Burt had now joined the convoy. I don't know if there were any more but it did seem a bit surreal as I ventured along the trail with a posse of riders chatting behind me. I wish I had been a bit more with it to appreciate those who had made the effort to see me. My body continued to weaken where every action and thought required an immense amount of energy.

Easy

Oh dear

By Simon Catmur

It's a sunny summer Saturday morning and I'm standing midway up Itford Hill, focussing on a South Down's Way signpost at the top of the hill, waiting.

It's dry, bright and still and I've cycled all of 4 miles from my house in Telscombe. I'm waiting to meet Richard Sterry and he's already cycled over 200 miles and is on the third and final leg of a 300mile South Downs Way Triple. We might be in the same National Park but we're not in the same ballpark. Richard's aiming to complete this ride in 36 hours, he's the first person to do this and he's welcome to it.

Then all of a sudden, it is him - my first sighting of the South Down 'Triplist', hurtling towards me with his support rider Simon Usher, only slowing to brake as the grass turned into a tight chalk & rocky camber.

I picked up my bike & took the short cut via Rodmell, climbed past the Dicklands and waited for him at the gate by the house on the hill.

I updated the Single Track World post with:

"He shot past with one support rider; now waiting outside Kiri Te Kanawa's house to see him again & maybe follow. By eck they look fast & fresh."

Here he comes again; head bobbing up the climb from Sh1t Farm. After a quick introduction I joined Richard on his ride and we headed towards Kingston Ridge. Barely 10 minutes in, and we lost Simon the support rider to a puncture. I was asked to stay with Richard and Simon would repair the flat and catch us up. We weren't to see Simon again for an hour or so as it happened, which gave us time to get acquainted.

We rode together up Newmarket Hill, turned left by Blackcap at the top of Lewes and were set fair for Ditchling Beacon. We had a nice little routine going where Richard would open the gates and I would close them; a little staccato perhaps but it worked and was easy to follow.

In fact 'easy' was probably how I'd sum up my ride with Richard so far; he was making this look easy and as long as he ate and drank regularly he looked nailed on to do this. Easy.

All I had to do was to remind Richard to re-fuel, keep him company and anticipate and deal with issues like horses, cows, other cyclist, walkers, dogs and the odd vehicle; the stuff you normally deal with subconsciously on the South Downs Way but exactly the sort of things that could cause issues for a rider who'd been riding solidly for the past 26 hours or so.

The pace was steady and we inched our way up New Timber Hill on the west side of the A23. The chalky single-track climb turns into a rutted grassy climb and you know that you've been on a climb by the time you reach the gate at the Sussex Border Path at the top. Richard wasn't thinking about that and he wanted me to push on ahead and advise his support crew that fresh coffee was being served in the café at a farm close to where they were meeting him at the bottom of the next descent. A tired person might not think about that or show that much concern; like I said, it all seemed a bit easy and I never got the sense that there was any impending difficulty.

We met Richard's support crew in the lay-by at the bottom of the climb to Devils Dyke and we met up again with Simon who'd fixed the puncture at Kingston Ridge and had been picked up.

Legs were massaged, health checks were made and Richard was re-fuelled and we were good to go. We were now joined by John Lemonius, Gavin Thomson and Jo Burt who had all been following Richard's progress on the Singletrack World feed. The conversation flowed and we giggled our way over the Dyke, along the escarpment and on towards Truleigh Hill. There is a super-fast chalky descent before the final climb to the towers at Truleigh Hill and I took up a position at the back to keep an eye on things and take in the view over the Weald to the right, Worthing and the Channel to the left and Chanctonbury Ring ahead – our next significant marker. The scenery looked fine; everything was in its right place, but Richard didn't look as sure footed as he had done earlier.

I moved closer to keep an eye on Richard on the final climb to the towers and it was obvious that he was struggling. His body had never cycled this long and this hard before and it was shaking its head at him.

The pace slowed on the level at the top and it was clear that our next target was going to be crucial to the success of the ride. We carefully dropped down the rutted track to the Adur River and met the support crew in the lay-by not a moment too soon. Richard was in trouble and the South Downs Triple was in jeopardy.

I think that we hung around that lay-by for almost an hour; sometimes acting as wind breaks for Richard and often huddled in a small group waiting and wondering. Richard was on his back for much of this time, wrapped in space blankets and thermals - taking in fluids and generally looking for all the world like his ride was over. There was little that we could do to help and our words of encouragement and our shows of empathy and concern were nullified when Richard was placed in one of the support vehicles and the sliding door was shut.

Oh dear.

Time passed and it was clear that a lot more time could pass before Richard would be able to continue - if he would or could continue at all. There was nothing else for us to do and we went on our separate ways, the ride was over. We didn't even get the chance to say 'good-bye' to Richard.

We may have been asked not to tweet, post or tell anyone about Richard's condition at the Adur but we were in no mood to even think about it anyway. I had a fairly numb ride home through Brighton and my thoughts were with Richard.

Only Richard can tell you what happened at the Adur, how his support team got him back on his bike and how he carried on to complete the triple because he's the only person to do it. And that makes his effort all the more special.

Downhill

Isn't the Double
or 24 hours enough?

The descent down Beeding Hill was terrifying. The other riders had all gone ahead of me and I was left alone, I felt so very alone. My wobbly arms struggled to keep the front wheel in the groove where a slight misjudgement would send me flying, as it did to a friend previously. Reaching the bottom I felt emotionally and physically drained.

Crossing the road to the car park I needed a lie down. Elevating my feet on the bumper of the van, I lay flat out on the tarmac. Rapidly my temperature plummeted to the point where Dr Jerry was rather concerned. Shivering in the sunlight, I was wrapped in space blankets and protected from the wind. Hearing the support crew talking firmly to a driver complaining about the position of some vehicles, I overheard them saying there was a medical emergency. In my confused state, I wondered what might have happened to one of the runners.

There was one thing I was not confused about, I had to keep going. "I've got to get to Amberley" I muttered to Anne as my lower lip trembled and my eyes rolled to the top of my head. Dave Brothers was coming down especially to see me at Bury, just beyond Amberley, and I didn't want to let him down. I hate letting people down.

Dr Jerry and Anne were seriously worried about my condition and contemplated on pulling me out of the event. The decision for me to stop on medical grounds would only be made by the medics, I had no say. If such a decision was called, I had agreed to respect their judgement. It was a moment I feared. It was also a promise made to my wife, Fiona, who was equally concerned for my safety.

The group of riders sheltered me from the cold wind as they wondered if I would get back on the bike. After a while their doubts increased and they went their separate ways. It was really nice of them to come and see me and must have felt disappointed that the South Downs Way had devoured another victim.

To warm me up I was moved into the shelter of the camper van and given a mug of tea. Replacing my wet top for something dryer and eating a cake, I began to feel a bit better. It's amazing what tea and cake can do.

Dr Jerry gave me some mental agility and memory tests that I think I passed quite well. My temperature was also increasing. Providing a urine sample, Dr Jerry checked for any protein or blood that would indicate signs of kidney damage. The tests were clear so Dr Jerry allowed me to get back on the bike if I wanted to. Of course I want to; I need to get to Winchester. I was now feeling a bit better in myself after the 50 minute rest.

Ant Jordon and Rachel Sokal had now joined the support crew with their much needed camper van. They provided a fresh boost to the tired team. Ant and Simon rode with me on the long climb up to Chanctonbury Ring. Focusing on the ride just to achieve the next few miles, my brain couldn't cope with much else. I let Ant and Simon do all the talking as I rode slightly ahead and opened the gates. My legs still felt OK, they just kept going, but it was the rest of me that was suffering.

Ant has a wealth of cycling experience and raced at the 24 World Championships in 2010. His enthusiasm and love of cycling provided a real boost to Simon who had been awake for a very long time. With my diminishing brain power, I just kept going with very few thoughts or emotions.

During the check point at Washington, I noticed a change in the support crew's behaviour. They no longer asked me what I wanted but just gave me food and drinks. They had taken over the decision making process, probably because I was giving incomprehensible answers to their questions. With their wealth of experience, I trusted their judgement and just did what I was told.

Setting short milestones we continued steadily on. Working on autopilot, I relied on the muscle memory for efficient pedalling technique and my intuition for navigation. Passing Amberley, I made it up the climb to the Bury road. Normally my tired legs would scream at the pain of riding up such a hill but they were beyond the pain barrier.

We had agreed to maintain 'Radio Silence' if anything went wrong so my family could be informed before hearing about any catastrophes on social media. Looking back it is interesting during this time of silence seeing the comments on the Singletrack World forum. There was clearly a buzz about my ride which was getting louder now that I was onto the third leg.

171. **piha**
> That is a monster effort, well done that man!

172. **john_l**
> Looks like he's just crossed the A24.
>
> Rode with him with a few others from Saddlescombe (up there) to the Adur   still smiling & riding well.
>
> Fantastic ride!

173. **squeekybrakes**
> Does anyone know if the Wessex way double (2x150 miles) has ever been attempted?

174. **grazedknees**
> Hi all. Just left Bury, all going well aside from GPS batteries so there's a new Endomondo route for you all. Follow Richard
> here http://www.endomondo.com/workouts/user/4762822

175. **smiff**
> haha great stuff. I might cheer him as he goes through QECP again this evening.
> I find this quite incredible, I have done the SDW a few times very slowly but I don't normally ride longer than 4 hours, can't imagine 36 hours... would definitely be asking for that Ass Cream after 6 or so and no longer able to steer a straight line in probably 12.

That extreme long distance stuff is a completely different sport. Is he enjoying it or just wanting to stop?

176. **muddy@rseguy**
Managed to catch up with Richard and two other support riders on the SDW from just before Chantry hill above Storrington to Amberley mount. He is seriously trucking along especially when you consider the distance already covered, looks very focused and obviously not wanting to chat. The group did say they really appreciate all the support that he's getting out on twitter and the Internet.

Mighty 😎

177. **Napalm**
Rode with Richard from Itford Hill to the Adur   seems focussed & calm. He's only going to go and do this isn't he?
The sun's out now & I'm full of cheese on toast. Richard says he's looking forward to a pint; reckon he's earned it. Godspeed.

178. **jimification**
Rode with him yesterday morning from Chanctonbury to Amberley. Glad to see he's still hammering along nicely! He's got the wind behind him now too.

179. **allthepies**
Not too far to go now, once he's cleared Butser then it's the home leg.

180. **muddy@rseguy**
Big apologies to all on SDW, I clean forgot to ask what tyres he is using. 😊

181. **m1kea**
Big apologies to all on SDW, I clean forgot to ask what tyres he is using.
Kenda Small Block from what I can read off my snaps 😆

Focus

I carried on in my ignorance

Dave Brothers had been waiting extremely patiently at Bury, it was very kind of him to come out and help, especially as he did not know me. The Endomondo had been reporting my progress for the past 30 hours and had apparently stopped. We set up a Samsung Galaxy Ace phone, which has a low running power consumption, and attached an external battery pack where the 4 x AA batteries were regularly replaced. Unsure whether it was the phone or the App, Rachel had downloaded Endomondo and very kindly donated her phone to continue the tracking process. I realised later that this was a major sacrifice for her as she is very rarely seen without her phone. Rachel had recently won the 24 Hours of Exposure, the European Championships, and travelled down from Nottingham to offer her experience and support. I didn't see much of her during my ride but I know that she was doing all the essential background stuff to keep the show in motion. Thanks Rachel.

Simon hung up his riding shoes to take charge of the support crew, while Ant and Dave followed me. I really can't remember much about this part. I kept pedalling, my legs weren't complaining, my speed was OK, I couldn't think very much and talking was an effort, so I just carried on in my own little world. I didn't think about whether I would make it or not, hypothetical thinking was a waste of energy. I just focused on getting to the place a few miles ahead. This is where huge amounts of determination are needed for long endurance rides. If there is no solid focus or will to finish, giving up is easy. Developing such mental strength during training is essential in seeing the ride through to the end.

Unknown to me at the time, there was just Ant following me as Dave had punctured after leaving Bury. He rapidly changed the tube then had to leg it to catch up with Ant and me. It was quite an effort he told me afterwards as were going at a fair pace. Although he only took a few minutes to fix the puncture, it seemed to take him ages to catch us up. If you know Dave, he's a fast rider and is regularly on the podium at races. I was honoured that Dave was prepared to help me for my ride and have since got to know him a bit more. There's something about the cycling community that unites us. Very few people knew me before my Triple, yet lots of riders wanted to come and see me and help out where possible. Thank you.

The field after Littleton Farm contained rape seed with a very narrow trail leading up the hill. With the recent heavy rain and warm temperatures, the crop was in abundance reaching shoulder height. Squeezing the handlebars between the branches, I was glad not to have bar ends which could easily have got caught and pulled me off. It was one of those sections that demanded all my concentration so I just gritted my teeth until it was over.

After what appeared an age I emerged out the other side to spend the next 3 miles picking the florets off the bike.

Reaching Cocking, the support crew were ready and waiting. There were a couple of supporters for the running event who had stayed behind to see me. Not wanting to disappoint them, I went over to say a quick hello and thanked them for their support. Oat cakes with honey were presented to me as I was fed the pieces like a small child.

Kate had taught me the art of efficient pedalling to the point where it came naturally. I didn't have to think about my legs they just kept on going applying the power to the pedals. It was on the long climb up past Cocking, I realised I wasn't that far from the QECP. Once past the park, Winchester isn't much further. The feeling that the end was approaching got me thinking. I might actually do it. I might actually become the first person to complete the South Downs Triple. I suddenly started to feel all emotional.

Flicking back into reality and realising that I had another 35 miles to go, I had to focus on the moment and the task of getting to the next check point.

Descending the chalky slope at Beacon Hill I saw a familiar person in Torq lycra. It was Lydia Gould and this time I recognised her. Joining in with Dave and Ant they all rode a few metres behind me, leaving me to bury myself in my thoughts. The problem was that I had no thoughts; I was very much in the zone where nothing around me mattered. I just had to keep the wheels turning.

Envelope 14 - Queen Elisabeth Country Park

Just keep me going

Approaching the QECP I realised that Butser Hill was the last real challenge before Winchester. Eager to get on at the check point, I got a bit impatient with the crew trying to stuff food down me. They could see that my energy levels were plummeting as I carried on in my ignorance.

There was another change in the support crew as they appeared to lose their sense of urgency to get me back on the trail. I got a bit frustrated as I was on a mission and needed to get going. They could see the deterioration in my body and wondered if I would make the next check point. This was their way of making sure that I was ready to continue.

Riding as far as I could up Butser, I used different muscles for the rest of the climb. Taking advantage of the general downward trend, I picked up speed for the next few miles. The bike continued to cruise along nicely as the trails appeared familiar. Rounding the corner at Whitewool Farm we came across a couple of riders battling with the chain gate. They had set out from

Eastbourne the previous day and wanted to get to Winchester before nightfall. Dave tactfully told them that I had also set out from Eastbourne the previous day and was also going to Winchester, again.

182.**spooky_b329**
Ha...I've been wondering why he's been stuck nr Bury the last few times I've checked Endomondo...got to change the day, doh!

183.**Shorty121**
Haha I made the same mistake 😜

184.**muddy@rseguy**
Looks like he's just about to go up Butser Hill, the last big climb of the day.

185.**allthepies**
Don't envy him that Butser climb but once done then he's homeward bound.

186.**dobo**
He maybe having a pitstop at QECP, that climbs a beast and maybe thinking he's almost home but there's still some hills to go and i hate to say it possibility of rain.

187.**dobo**
He's over Butser, I bet that one hurt, looks like he's just trucking on again!

188.**allthepies**
Looked like a push up Butser from the speed but he's crested it now!

189.**dobo**
Maybe spun out on a granny but if he's sensible he walked 😜 last thing he needs is to go anaerobic up a huge hill during a 300 mile endurance event 😊

190.**nosherduke996**

I am from the same cycle club as Richard and there is no way he will walk any of it.

191.**allthepies**

nosherduke996 said *» I am from the same cycle club as Richard and there is no way he will walk any of it.*

After over 250 miles and faced with a very steep hill he may not have any say in the matter 😃

192.**grazedknees**

A quick update from the support crew - he's left QE2 and going great guns. We're happy cos the cafe was open and we've all had tea 😃
Follow him here...
http://www.endomondo.com/workouts/user/4762822

193.**dobo**

I think he's sped up? Clearly he should be doing 4 laps 😊

194.**nosherduke996**

After over 250 miles and faced with a very steep hill he may not have any say in the matter

This guy is a machine. He even goes out with the roadies on his MTB and can average 16mph.

Close to Home

Nightfall was approaching
for the second time during the ride

Stopping briefly at the divide for the 2009 Temporary South Downs Way route, I didn't need anything and wanted to carry straight on. Simon took me to one side saying that there would be an extra check point at the Milburys pub. Thinking that the support crew were desperate for another beer, I didn't complain as they had deserved it and I just wanted to get myself to Winchester. Simon then explained the reason for the extra stop. He spoke very calmly and reassuringly and for a moment I feared the worst. He said that at the pub waiting for me was Fiona and my 17 year old children Lorna and Dan. I couldn't believe that Fiona had driven the 80 miles to come and see me. She never came to see me ride my bike, she never appeared to show any interest in my cycling, yet now she had broken the mould to see me achieve something amazing. I tried unsuccessfully to contain my emotions. Then Simon added a bit more. Dan, he said, was all kitted out with his bike and would ride the last bit with me into Winchester. Hastily I got back on the trail before my emotions got the better of me. It was so unexpected and such an overwhelming surprise, I could hardly contain myself.

Previously when training for big events, they consumed all my thoughts and energy to the detriment of family life causing Fiona to lose interest in my cycling.

Fiona did join me for a bike ride once, it was a fun his and hers 2 up time trial organised by Redhill Cycling Club. She borrowed my old road bike and tootled around the course with me providing encouragement from my mountain bike. This didn't spark a desire for her to ride again so she maintained her distance from the two wheeled machines.

Fiona had only found out about my Triple ride about two weeks previously. She knew I was preparing for a big ride and assumed it was a race of some sort. She didn't think it was that big as I was still doing things around the house. Apparently she can tell when I'm planning something big, as it absorbs all my attention and everything else goes to pot. I hadn't told her earlier about the Triple as I didn't think she was interested.

"So you're doing the South Downs Way three times?" she asked casually when I mentioned the Triple.

"Yes" I replied and waited with baited breath for her reaction.

"OK" was the apparently apathetic response as she continued eating her dinner. Was that all? OK? Doesn't she realise the incredible challenge I'm about to do? The conversation was changed to something else as we continued eating.

Arriving home from work the next day, I was greeted with the phrase

"We need to talk!"

Uh oh!

Fiona was naturally concerned for my safety and asked all the caring questions. I reassured her about the medics on the support crew and invited her to the next planning session where she could meet the support crew and Dr Jerry. All her concerns were put to rest when she realised the experience of the support crew. Staying on to enjoy Campari Cocktails and a meal she gained complete trust in the support crew.

Baking loads of cakes for the crew and asking if I needed anything specific to eat, Fiona was fully involved with the event. It was so reassuring at last to have my family on side, hence my emotional reaction when I heard they were coming to see me.

Fiona's visit was due to be a surprise for me but given my state of mind, such a surprise might have been too much. Therefore the decision to tell me just beforehand seemed appropriate and worked out well.

Racing down to Exton I sped along the hard bumpy mud and wove around the fields. Reaching the disused railway line, I accelerated off leaving Dave and Ant to catch me up. Fiona, Lorna & Dan were going to be at the next check point. The thought wouldn't leave my head.

Climbing the long road out of Exton was a slog. It was long and probably quite slow, all I could hear was Dave and Ant chatting away behind me. I tried to focus. For the first time I couldn't think what was coming up next on the trail. I knew there was a farm, a road and a field but I couldn't put them in order. A sense of panic filled my mind, then I realised that this was wasting valuable energy. I just had to work on the moment and get myself through each bit at a time. This was mentally the toughest part of the ride, my mind was fading fast and I knew it. All my mental techniques were exhausted. What's more, I could feel my shoulders rocking, a classic sign of a weak core. I could feel my body giving up on me again but I wouldn't let it. Having got so close, failure was not an option. I was going to get to Winchester.

My mum has always shown strong support for my riding challenges. She studies my plans to a great extent and comes up with a very different perspective identifying something I may have missed. This time she was thinking about the Jubilee celebrations in case any of the street parties might restrict the movements of the support crew, as they entered Winchester.

Whilst writing this book I asked my parents to check a draft version. They were horrified to discover the impact such endurance rides had on the body and how much the mental state deteriorates. Since my Triple, although they are still supportive, they do keep reminding me that I'm not as young as I used to be.

The road was relentless, appearing twice as long as it should be. As we turned to climb up towards the trig point, the heavens opened. Ant had a waterproof ready for me while Dave went on to announce our arrival. It was a yellow waterproof! Everything else was colour coordinated to be red and black; my bike, my clothes, my gloves and my helmet. Apparently I had been given the yellow top as Dan was wearing my red one. If my brain wasn't struggling to exist I might have kicked up a fuss, but at this stage I was glad of some shelter from the heavy rain.

The weather up until this point had been brilliant. The trails were bone dry and there was no mud to be seen. In case you are wondering, this was in 2012 just before the two months of torrential rain in June and July. In some ways this rain didn't matter, in my current state I had no thoughts or feelings towards it; I just had to get to Winchester. A bit of rain here was not going to stop me.

Simon Usher @dadwithabike
#sd3 **One more official checkpoint and a sneeky pub stop before final run into Winchester.** @hillburner **- 35 hours and still going** #awesome

the Real BeerBiker @BeerBiker
Sitting at Milburys in Beauworth waiting for @hillburner #SD3 **with a lovely pint of 3 Spires. Just 7 miles to go to make history :-))**

Tony Walden @tonywalden13
@hillburner **an amazing ride so far, I doff my cap to you sir, head down for the final leg**

Pat Sterry @PatSterry
@dadwithabike @hillburner **Nearly there. Keep going. M&D**

Steve Golding @stevegolding2#sd3 @hillburner **Rich this is your time. You need to grasp it with both hands and push for that finish line. You can do this. Come on dude.**

Jo Burt @VecchioJo
hurry up @hillburner, **i want my supper!! :-)**

Tucking my head down to avoid the downpour, I carried on to the Milburys pub. Seeing my car in the car park completely confused me. Why was it here? I had left it at home and the tank was low on petrol. It was like in a dream where something completely out of context appears on the scene.

I then saw Fiona, Lorna and Dan huddled under a parasol and guessed they had used my car to get here.

Fiona had contacted the support crew around lunchtime suggesting her idea of the family coming to see me. At this point I was laid out on the car park near Steyning with the support crew seriously doubting if I would finish the ride. When I was back on the bike they replied to Fiona for her to drive down to the Milburys Pub. Back at home there was the struggle to get Dan's bike into Fiona's car so she grabbed my larger car, and then found the tank was empty.

I managed to say a quick hello and made sure Dan was ready to ride the last bit with me. Quite why I was checking on Dan I'm not sure as the support crew were far more capable than me.

Apart from meeting the family at the Milburys Pub there was another reason for the additional check point. The support crew were really worried about me as it didn't look as though I would be able to make it to Winchester. They wanted to keep a close eye on me at this final stage. In my mind I had no doubts of completing the Triple and I didn't know what all the fuss was about, but the outward signs from my body were telling a very different story.

Simon handed me a For Goodness Shake to help start my recovery process. It went down with ease just like the others I had taken during the ride. The For Goodness Shake people had kindly sent me a load of drinks for my ride and recovery. I tend to use their products quite a bit, so their donation was most welcome – thanks.

After confirming the place where Dan would ride the final descent, we set off with lights ablaze. Nightfall was approaching for the second time during the ride.

Conscious of time I raced along the flatter section towards Holden Farm. It was 8.20pm and a part of my brain was functioning where I realised that I could try for a sub 37 hour time. This meant finishing by 9pm. The original target was 36 hours whereas I now thought that 36:59 would appear a lot better than 37:01.

Remembering to do the two sides of the triangle for the official South Downs Way route by Ganderdown Farm, we ploughed on as fast as my legs would allow. A large herd of cows clogged up the trail in one of the fields. Various tactics were used to disperse them so we could get through.

195.**cinnamon_girl**
How are the weather conditions there?

196.**m1kea**
Looks like late teens temps and the easterly wind continues.
Now on last major climb.

197.**cinnamon_girl**
Old Winchester Hill done and dusted.

198.**richen987**
Pretty much there, amazing ride, hats off to the fellow

199.**weeksy**
Wow.... impressed. Been out all day at Fod... so not seen the updates.
Respect to the guy.

200.**Matt24k**

His average speed is going up. Has he got a lead out man for the sprint finish? 😃
Keep going, the end is in sight.

201.**cinnamon_girl**

Yep just crossing the A272. That's my old riding territory!

202.**allthepies**

Nearly at Cheesefoot Head, downhill from there 😃

203.**cinnamon_girl**

Go Richard go!

204.**dobo**

Good job he's using Endomondo and not Strava otherwise he'd be shouting STRAVA RUN SDW triple KOM!!! Open that gate!!!

205.**higthepig**

Been watching it on Endomondo at work, extremely addictive, chapeau to him, stunning effort.

206.**theotherjonv**

I'm absolutely and totally stunned by this. I've done the SDW in 2 days, and have ambitions to do it in one day.
Buy him a pint from me when he finishes

207.**cinnamon_girl**

So close!

208.**Matt24k**

How close is so close in miles?

209.**allthepies**

Minutes away! Just over a mile.

210.**cinnamon_girl**

Dunno the route through to Winch, couple of miles?

211.m1kea
Last mile or so of road to do now

212.Matt24k
He'll probably get nicked for riding with no rear light!

Crossing the road at Cheesefoot Head the mud was becoming slippery. I wanted to push on hard but Ant kept telling me to take it easy and focus on the trail. I knew this part well; turn right, follow it through the trees, along the side of the field and down the hill. It's not very far but it went on for ages. Puddles were forming as the rain continued to pour. "Take it easy" came Ant's voice again. I so wanted to push on harder but realised these were wise words. The trail just kept on going; I was still riding along the side of the field and the descent was yet to come.

Eventually we hit the track, passed the house and joined the road. Ant was probably still telling me to take it easy but by this stage he was out of earshot as I sped down the hill. I needed to get to Winchester.

Reaching the main road I followed the cycle track that passes the entrance to the cricket club. Dan was ready and waiting as he tucked in behind us. Dave had gone on ahead to announce our imminent arrival while Ant checked that Dan was OK.

We sped up the final climb of the day on to the bridge over the M3 and found Petersfield Road leading into Winchester. Slipping into the big ring I didn't spare the horses. Judging by their lights, Dan and Ant were not too far behind. And yes, I did have a rear light, Simon made sure one was fitted when I stopped at the pub.

The goal of the South Downs Triple was nearly mine. The months of relentless training and preparation had paid off. I was going to do it. I was going to prove all the sceptics wrong.

The road at the bottom was clear as I headed right to reach the roundabout. Standing on the pedals with my legs still feeling strong, I veered left at the roundabout to see King Alfred's statue. The end was in sight.

A cheer went up from the support crew and my family as I reached my destination.

I stopped pedalling.
I didn't need to pedal any more.
I had finished and I was finished.

Photos were hastily taken with the timing clock at 21:04 on 2nd June 2012. The 300 miles were completed in 37:04 hours.

213.singletrackmind
In Winch town I reckon all done bar the champagne.

214.dobo
yep, looks like he's there! Amazing top challenge!

215.ackie
I think congratulations are in order.
Amazing achievement Richard!

216.cinnamon_girl
Stonking performance Sir, well done! 😃

217.jimification
Fantastic!

218.avdave2

219.drofluf
Awesome!

220.CaptJon

221.allthepies
Awesome achievement!

222.Napalm

Super human.

223.nosherduke996

He is now riding back home before it gets dark.

224.m1kea

Well done Mr S.

225.Matt24k

First man on the moon. First 4 minute mile. First SDW Triple.
No one can ever take that away.
Well done Richard and the whole team.

226.jimification

Yes, his backup team looked incredibly well organised. Reckon they did a superb job.

227.flebby

228.giqles

Incredible achievement. Congratulations!

229.muddy@rseguy

Awesome job, well done

230.superfli

Top marks, well done Richard! And excellent support too

231.chiefgrooveguru

Awesome!

232.nuke

Superb! Well done Richard

233.cyclistm

Incredible effort. Humbling even..

234.**faz083**

Insane effort, nice one 😃

235.**brooess**

Smashing. Huge effort. Chapeau!

236. muppetWrangler

Congratulations.

237.**Mostly Balanced**

He is now riding back home before it gets dark.
He doesn't live in Eastbourne does he?
Cracking effort.

238.**composite**

Well done Richard!
Spent the last 36 hours watching Endomondo like it was live TV coverage. It was strangely compelling!
Any confirmation on the final time?

239.**grazedknees**

Yes final time 37 hours and 4 minutes.
It was an absolute pleasure being part of the 1st South Downs Triple team. Richard was amazing. That is all.

240.**cinnamon_girl**

Of course well done to the support crew, there would have been some challenging logistics involved too!
How is he feeling?

241.**corroded**

Mind boggling ride. Very pleased Richard made it.
Been following from Australia but I've ridden much of SDW but no way could I imagine doing it three times in one go!!

Louise Poynton @DirtDiva48
@Anne24solo @hillburner **well done Rich, just before the rain came pouring down! Amazing effort.x**

Neil @compositeone
Well done @hillburner **completing the first SDW triple! Spent the last 36 hours watching Endomondo like it was live TV strangely compelling!**

Judy @beer_babe
#sd3 **Incredible achievement by** @hillburner **on his 37h 04m SD triple. Honoured to have been part of the team. Now I need some sleep!!**

mtbJim @mtbJim69
@hillburner **Wey hey!! Well done you. Amazing!!**

ashleygreen14 @ashleygreen14
@Pricycles #sd3 **A guy just rode the South Downs Way 3x starting 8am Friday and finished 9pm Saturday. All over now but stunning.**

Stuart Brierley @Stu_at_Tesla
@hillburner **I rode with you when you did the SDW double.....never knew you'd go for the triple! AWESOME!**

Steve Golding @stevegolding2
@hillburner #sd3 **Fantastic riding. Been a pleasure to watch you achieve this. Congrats to you and your Team. Good to see you on the downs.**

jim russell @jimification
@hillburner **Woooopp! He's done it!!!!! Guessing it's raining in Winch too - proper epic finish to an monster of an epic ride - congrats!**

Ben Hunt-Davis @BenHuntDavis6 Jun
@hillburner many many congrats to Richard on being
the 1st to do the South Downs triple.
http://richardsterry.blogspot.co.uk/
37hrs on a bike nonstop!!!!

John McFaul @JohnMcFaul
Hats off to @hillburner for his South Downs Triple in
37 hrs. That's 300 miles of there and back and there
again. Incredible. Crazy though.

Envelope 15 - Winchester

We did it

Beyond the End

Finished

There was no energy left in me to scream

Many stories of heroic achievements usually end at this point. The goal has been accomplished, everyone is celebrating and they all live happily ever after.

This bit is about what happened next. It was very strange for me and totally unexpected.

The support crew were jubilant telling everyone in the vicinity about the amazing achievement. Words of congratulations came flooding in from those in the nearby pub and the local students, who had probably just been in the pub, but I felt nothing. I had no sense of excitement or victory; in fact I couldn't find any emotions. All the celebrations seemed a bit distant. For the past 37 hours I had been pretty much alone on my bike, and now the peace and tranquillity was shattered.

I needed a few moments to unwind to try to absorb what I had done. As my legs surprisingly still felt good, perhaps I should have got back on the bike and ridden gently for a couple of miles with no pressure of hills or time. Sadly this didn't happen as I didn't have the means to gather or convey my feelings. The frenzy of activity around me muddled my few remaining thoughts.

The medics took control guiding me into the van and packing ice blocks around my legs. Simon had arranged for me to change in the pub using a prepared bag of fresh clothes. Downing a For Goodness Shake to help the recovery process, another bottle was provided for my journey home.

I struggled to say a few words to all my supporters who had helped be achieved my goal. I wanted to thank everyone individually for their unique contribution and commitment, but words were not my strong point. In fact nothing was my strong point and I was fit for nothing.

The next thing I remember was being squashed up in my car trying to navigate for Fiona to drive us out of Winchester. Feeling tired and exhausted, my legs began to hurt as I couldn't stretch them out in the car. The journey appeared to last forever, all I wanted to do was to snuggle into bed and sleep.

Reaching home an hour later, Dan took control.

"Put on these 3 T shirts and this hoodie" he said in a very authoritative manner as he filled the bath with cold water. I was in no position to argue with my son, as thinking for myself was just not possible. I carefully eased myself into the painfully chilling water and then Dan proceeded to open 2 large bags of ice that he poured in around my legs. There was no energy left in me to scream, I just sat and shivered in a dazed state.

 Dan Sterry @DanSterry
@hillburner #SD3 **At home now he's sitting in ice bath, shall we leave him there all night!?**

Then, after warming up in a cool shower, I finally crawled into bed falling into a deep sleep.

The Day After

I slept, I got up,
I ate, I slept,
I ate some more,
I went back to bed.

Waking at 7am the next morning I went downstairs. My legs were fine with no aches or pains, obviously the ice had done its stuff.

Trying to make a cup of tea I crashed around in the kitchen as I had lost all sense of coordination. Checking my hands, I couldn't feel my fingers. My left arm couldn't even lift its own weight. The extreme duration of the ride had damaged the nerves and caused some muscle wastage in my arms. Coordinating my hands just to lift a teaspoon was a mighty effort.

Sitting on the sofa with some breakfast, I pondered about the past 48 hours. I had achieved my goal, the goal of a lifetime, but it didn't feel like an achievement. It didn't feel like anything special. I didn't feel anything. I know it can take a while for the realisation of the moment to arrive, but these feelings of nothing went on for weeks. I comforted myself saying it was not about the goal, but it's the journey that's important. I had enjoyed the journey in the form of the preparations, and the journey of the Triple itself.

It was a couple of days after my Double ride in 2009 when I suddenly realised what I had just done. The emotions welled up inside of me and I felt elated that I had achieved something incredible. I guess I was looking for something similar after the Triple, but nothing happened.

Josh Ibbett wrote a really nice piece on the USE (Exposure Lights) web site that helped, and there was a short article in the local paper.

Later I discovered a wonderful blog post by Ben Hunt-Davis who had studied my blog and wrote his own summary.

My stomach appeared relatively normal afterwards, despite consuming 33 gels and countless litres of energy drink. Huge cravings for protein followed as I dug out a large pack of sausages from the freezer.

242.**grazedknees**

He did it 😊
Woken up this morning and if I am this knackered (but elated) I have no idea how Richard is feeling :)))))))
Hope he enjoyed his ice bath!

243.**Sandwich**

He'll be walking like John Wayne for a day or two. Chapeau.

246.**offthebrakes**

Surprised you've emerged from bed this early Anne

247.**beacon2**

Forgive me for joining this thread a bit late, but I've been out riding my bike for the last couple of days.

Yes, the South Downs Triple was an insane and crazy idea to most, but to me it was challenging and awesome.

It was tough, very tough in places, however I stayed focused and just got on with the ride.

The support crew was amazing and it has just taken me a couple of hours to read through all your posts and tweets. I had no idea of the volume of your virtual support.

I'll be posting more information later on http://richardsterry.blogspot.co.uk/ to tell you more about the ride.

It would be great for a couple of charities to benefit from my efforts;
The British Heart Foundation who originally inspired me to ride the SDW in a day, back in 2007.
St Marys Church, Reigate who are building a new Community Centre
http://www.justgiving.com/teams/southdownstriple

Thanks again for your support and encouragement.

It was after lunch on the first day when the tiredness hit me. I slept, I got up, I ate, I slept, I ate some more, I went back to bed. Being up all night can take a few days to catch up on sleep, riding all day, all night, and then all day again takes a lot longer to catch up on sleep. I lived in a zombie-like state where I was too tired to do anything yet sleeping twice a day. The longer it dragged on the more frustrated I got. This real tiredness lasted two to three weeks and it was over a month before any form of activity wasn't followed by a huge desire to rest.

What next? Was a question that I was asked repeatedly just after completing my Triple ride. I think the questioner is wondering what sort of challenge I might aim for, to top what I have just achieved. Struggling to answer this, my frustration was twofold. Firstly, didn't they think that I'd achieved enough, showing no respect to my existing accomplishment and think that I needed to go on and do something better? Secondly, they clearly didn't understand the dramatic impact the Triple had on my body and the risks involved, and they wanted me to do it and more again?

I got to the point where I declined to answer the question. I was still recovering from the Triple, which was a goal in itself.

Bit by bit I tried to piece things back together. The weekly physio sessions helped to repair the nerves in my hand. As the nerves regained some feeling the pains in my hand were at times excruciating. Six weeks later when some of the pain had subsided, whilst on holiday I ventured out on a bike for the first time. It was great to be back on two wheels again and everything was going well. Taking an off road descent the jars from the hired bike with rather stiff forks, shot straight up my arm bringing the pain right back. Griping the bars became a mighty effort and braking was virtually impossible. I made an unscheduled dismount as I hit the deck.

Staying off the bike I volunteered as a Dog Handler for the Big Dog bike race near Brighton. It was fantastic to be involved and I thoroughly enjoyed helping out with the event. There was also an opportunity to see and thank those who had come out to meet me on my ride.

11 weeks after the Triple I ventured out on my bike. It was a wonderful feeling to be riding again. Simon had kindly cleaned the bike after the Triple ride, so it was mud free and gleaming. My left hand tingled slightly when holding the bars, so I took it easy and stayed on the road.

Incidentally, whilst preparing the bike for this ride, I removed a thorn from the front tyre. Helping the Slime to do its stuff no further action was needed. I don't know where I picked up the thorn, but if it had been on the final leg of the Triple I would have found it a real struggle to change the tube. The reason for the Slime not working when I punctured on the first mile was due to the slow wheel speed whilst climbing the first hill, the slime had not had time to spread out around the tube. In hindsight, if I had rotated the wheel so the puncture was at the bottom, the Slime may have done its stuff and I wouldn't have needed to change the tube.

Three months after my Triple ride with my hand better, I ventured off road with some friends on the South Downs. It was great. The freedom, the bumps, the speed and the adrenalin were awesome.

As the winter weather closed in and work pressures increased, I lost the motivation to carry on riding. Previous winter training was always in preparation for a target event in the summer. I struggled to find a goal for 2013, how do you top the South Downs Triple? Even my original long term goal of wanting to get on the podium had evaporated. I was left with a sense of emptiness and a lack of purpose.

My body would not physically be able to cope with another long endurance event and the lack of winter training would not give me the endurance capability. I fought for a long time in trying to find a goal, then I realised it was staring me right in the face. After four years of rigorous training programmes focused towards challenging events, it was now time to turn things upside down. My goal was simple, to just enjoy riding and go with the flow. This doesn't fit in with any SMART objectives but my aim is to give my body a rest and give something back to the cycling community.

Once I had made this discovery, everything improved and I was desperate to get back out on the bike. The mental healing process was over and I could now move on with my life.

And the Winner is...

"There is only one clear winner for this award where many of us would struggle even to complete a third of what he has done." announced the chairman, Adrian Webb, to Redhill Cycling Club.

The annual awards ceremony had gone up a notch from an informal gathering to a smart dinner with a World Class Mountain Bike racer and potential Paralympic athlete presenting the prizes.

The award of "Peter's Golden Bicycle" relates back to when Peter King was part of the Redhill Cycling Club. Peter went on to become the Chief Executive of British Cycling who was at the helm for the 2008 Beijing Olympics. His achievement was rewarded with a CBE in 2009.

Each year Peter's Golden Bicycle is awarded to the club member who has excelled themselves on an endurance event.

"The winner of this award" continued Adrian "is someone who managed to cycle 300 miles and climb 36,000 feet in a time of 37 hours."

I felt slightly embarrassed being talked about in such a prestigious way surrounded by 80 club athletes.

"For achieving the South Downs Triple, the Winner is ... Richard Sterry"

Making my way up to the front of the room amongst a hearty applause I received the prize from good friend Anne Dickins.

Anne played a major part in the support for my ride and has since been selected for the Paralympic squad for Rio 2016. It was very fitting that Anne was able to present me with this award.

Final Thoughts

The South Downs Triple was a fantastic adventure; it consumed my thoughts for a year and gave my training an immense target to aim for. Building up to the ride I was amazed by the support from friends, for a superb support crew and to the many that followed my progress on the ride. I set out to achieve a personal goal and I'm delighted that so many others were able to join in and become part of the story.

Thank you for all your support. I still consider myself as 'just an ordinary bloke' who had a crazy idea. I hope this book helps to explain how to turn a crazy idea into reality. The supporters on the day turned the crazy challenge into a wonderful journey and a lasting memory.

Adrian Webb, chairman of Redhill CC, summed it up quite well by saying;

"Richard Sterry's South Downs Triple,
but he only went and did it!"

What they said

Exposure Lights News Item

By Josh Ibbett - www.exposurelights.com
South Downs Double record holder 17:47 hours

The South Downs Double has long been an iconic target for long distance cyclists. The 200 miles from Winchester to Eastbourne and back again has become a medal of honour for all who have been successful.

One such rider is Richard Sterry. He completed the Double in a time of 23 hours 31 minutes back in 2009, a fantastic achievement by any standards. This was not enough though!

As more and more riders completed the challenge and the record time tumbled Richard sat at home thinking how the bar could be raised. His answer was the Triple, Eastbourne to Winchester and back again and then back again! 300 miles in total of continual rolling hills, brutal!

So over the Jubilee holiday weekend Richard set out on his challenge:

"I paused for a moment. This was going to be the ride of my life, where I only had one chance to do the South Downs Triple. I noted all the important things that needed to be done in the next few hours before the ride, then made my decision."

Richard made a fantastic effort completing the ride in 37 hours 4 minutes and Exposure Lights are proud to have helped light the way.

Turning Crazy Goals into Reality:

By Ben Hunt-Davis
www.hunt-davis.co.uk

How Richard Sterry reached his big Triple goal by breaking it down into the Everyday.

Ben Hunt-Davis has competed at three Olympic Games, winning an Olympic Gold Medal at the Sydney Olympics in 2000 for rowing. He was lucky enough to be part of the staff of Team GB at London 2012. Since retiring from sport, Ben has worked with numerous organisations as a motivational speaker.

Richard's and Ben's paths crossed briefly in 2002 causing a profound effect on Richard's outlook in life and motivating him to take up cycling. Ten years later Richard surpassed the multitude to ride into the record books.

Breaking down long term goals

The other day I heard from a guy called Richard Sterry who had achieved the Triple – cycling across the South Downs non-stop 3 times – that's there and back 3 times. Some feat! And it got me thinking about how we can achieve long term goals.

It took him 37 and a bit hours – its 300 miles – 34,700 feet of hill climbing over 37 hours on a bike. His blog is great – he relates how hard it was in blow by blow detail, with challenges including a puncture in the first mile, but how he got by setting small steps and kept pushing himself. It's a pretty good read!

And then I read another blog on the subject by Anne Dickins, herself a very successful cyclist who raced in the 2010 World 24 hour Solo Mountain Bike Championships – her story was told from a different angle.

I found it a really interesting take on Richard's incredible feat. She talked about how meticulous he had to be in his planning for this – how he had to train whilst holding down a job, being a father, having a family and all those other things that most of us have to do in the day to day course of our lives. She describes him as being a "spreadsheet king" and how he looked at everything in huge amounts of detail and for ages beforehand. The thing he had in his mind all the while was this crazy goal of doing the Triple – something that nobody had ever done before.

Turning crazy goals into reality

He made it by focussing on the everyday layer that Harriet and I talk about in our book "Will it make the boat go faster?" in the chapter on Goals – the things he was doing on a daily basis that were taking him in the direction he wanted to go – and planning, planning, planning.

So often, we have goals we think about, some of them we might think about as being crazy and, by definition, almost impossible – others might be more normal. But often we fail to break down into the control layer, the concrete goal, and then into the everyday layer which is the sequence of small steps we need to take every day to make it happen.

How much time are you spending on the everyday layer? Are you breaking your big goals down in the way that Richard did – where every single day you are moving forward towards that goal by getting the small things done?

South Downs Way Triple 2012

By Judy McNeill
www.beerbabe.co.uk

There were 2 major events planned for the June 2012 bank holiday weekend: the Diamond Jubilee celebrations for Queen Elizabeth II and, more importantly, the South Downs Way Triple attempt by Richard Sterry. Richard (@Hillburner) was planning to complete 3 consecutive lengths of the South Downs Way on his mountain bike. Why?

Roy and I knew about the attempt and were planning to ride on the South Downs Way to meet up with him and maybe ride a short distance with him as motivation. However, things changed on Thurs 31st May at 12.49! I received the following Twitter DM from Anne Dickins:

31 May at 12:49

Hi judy, are u free tomo and or sat? Could you poss help us with sdw pit crew? Weather means we have moved it and we need new helpers?

I had little doubt about the answer but I confirmed with Roy and got straight back to Anne - we were in the team.

The alarm went off at 5am on the Friday morning and with a bowl of porridge inside, Roy drove me over to meet up with Richard Sterry and Simon Usher. The 3 of us then headed down to Eastbourne for the 8 am start. During the drive I was given my instructions and got myself ready.

It was a gloriously sunny day as we wound up Richard's elastic band and sent him on his way. Simon and I got the van ready while we waited for a courier to deliver the team T-shirts. They failed to do this so we headed off knowing we needed to make alternate arrangements to get them.

The months of planning that had been done had identified suitable 'check point' locations for us to meet up with Richard. Here we could replenish his supplies and also record all of the stats that would allow us to monitor his performance. I was given the responsibility for writing all this down.

Richard had worked out the average speed that he would need to maintain to;

1.   Improve his personal best for doing the Double
2.   Achieve his target for the Triple of 36 hours.

I also had to keep reminding him what the average speed needed to be to hit that target.

The last time I had done anything like this was the mid-1980's when Roy and I used to take part in stage rallies. We were both co-drivers/navigators and this would involve getting our drivers or the service crew to the required point at the required time. Things haven't really changed much except for the technology. I still love OS Maps.

So we met Richard at Firle, A27, Saddlescombe, Washington, Bury, Cocking, Queen Elizabeth CP, Milburys and, all too soon, we were in Winchester.

Leg 1 complete at 18.10 and time to turn around. Anne had joined us at QECP on the way down and Roy joined us on the way back. Anne had the motor home and Roy, the pocket rocket, our little C1 which he used to zip around and see Richard at additional points. He was responsible for the 99 ice cream at Ditchling Beacon on the final leg.

To keep the support team's spirits up, Richard gave us a number of envelopes which were to be opened at set check points. Simon and I spent ages at Saddlescombe trying to make paper planes and one envelope contained torches in readiness for the hours of darkness.

The best one was the 'recovery' box full of goodies that we opened when we got to Winchester for the first time.

We made Simon and Roy get some sleep during the second leg but unfortunately, we had to get them to 'rescue' us when the battery went flat on the chase van. It did mean that we all got to enjoy a close encounter with a herd of cows in the fog on top of Firle Beacon. They were crowding by the gate and we were concerned that they would get in Richard's way. I tried my hand at 'cow whispering' with the calves but only one of them decided to come close to me.

Richard reached Eastbourne at 06.55 - with a PB time of 22hr 55min for 2 legs. We located our T-shirts (in the grit bin of the local school) and were joined by Dr Jerry. The Triple had not been done before and it was not known what effect on the body it would have. At this point I had been awake for 26 hours straight.

Simon rode with Richard to Firle Beacon while the rest of us went by road - via a petrol station where we got sausage and bacon rolls. Mmmmm!

We managed to keep Richard going through the dark times he experienced through the next few check points. He was joined by other riders who were able to encourage him along his way although he didn't like too much chat or crowding.

Rachel Sokal and Ant Jordan met us at Steyning - where it looked as though we had reached the end of the attempt. They had been involved in all the planning and were originally going to do some of the roles that Roy and I filled, except Ant was due to ride more with Richard.

By the time we reached Steyning, I had been on the go for 31 hours and had mentally prepared myself to see it through to the end. I didn't really want to stop what I was doing. I wanted this to go on to Winchester.

But, at Steyning, we were also faced with the fact that Richard might not be able to go on. As he lay on the blanket on the ground, covered with more blankets...step up Dr Jerry and Anne!

Richard Sterry, a man barely alive...but we can rebuild him...we have the capability to make the world's first bionic man... better than he was before... better... faster... stronger...

And he was. He rode into Winchester at 21.04 - 3 legs completed in 37hrs and 4 minutes. 1st rider to ever do this. A world record!

And what did I do? I blubbed like a little baby! I was tired and emotional but I had had a great time. It was incredible to be part of such an amazing achievement.

Richard was a total star and what a machine. There are not enough words to describe what he had done. I could only aspire to being able to doing a small part of what he did - but maybe I have picked up a few tips from what I witnessed.

Post Script: at the end of the ride, Richard's Garmin showed 34,730 feet of climbing. That's 5,700 feet more climbing than the height of Everest, and in 37hrs 04mins! Puts things into perspective doesn't it!

The key to the success; comprehensive planning, a good support team, having a doctor & a physio around, support of friends and strangers, and hours of training.

Please don't try this at home........

.......The South Downs Triple

By Anne Dickins
www.annedickins24.blogspot.co.uk

"I want to be the first person to cycle the South Downs Way Triple, what do you think?"

Richard looked at me earnestly. Inside I was struggling to know how to respond Yer, yer, funny joke. Only 25% of people who attempt the Double have achieved it and Richard isn't your normal elite athlete.....

He was still looking at me intently and I realised he was being serious – and he wanted an answer.

"Really?" I said "Sure – why not!" He smiled and I realised that he had already decided he was going to do it. He was just testing me to see if I would be there for the journey.

The rulebook for the South Downs double hall of fame states that there are 2 categories - supported or unsupported – yes some people do the 200-mile double unsupported. Riding 300 miles off road in one go? Slightly crazy in its self, but to ride it unsupported would be crazy verging on dangerous. As the team came together we all wanted Richard to achieve his goal, but understanding the seriousness of his challenge we wanted to make sure that no one got hurt in the process – neither Richard, who was clearly at risk, nor any of the crew, who would also be getting fatigued driving for 36 hours on public roads. This was going to be a supported ride and, having some experience of 24-hour endurance racing and some personal experience at things going wrong, I volunteered along with Simon to coordinate the support.

That conversation was 15 months ago and last weekend he set off from Eastbourne to attempt to ride the South Downs Way three times in one go - 300 miles nonstop, including 30,000 feet of climbing, in a target time of 36 hours.

Richard is a planner, dare I say the spreadsheet king. He likes to know everything in advance to the minutest detail. Over the next 15 months he updated his massive file from his previous Double achievement with information on the challenge. Photos of every gate and junction, average prevailing winds, every checkpoint with an aerial view, and the location of 24hour supermarkets for emergency supplies for the crew or for if things weren't going to plan. Each check point had instructions of what he wanted, his nutrition, his clothing, his desired average mph – even when to text his wife! Every situation and possible problem had been thought through with contingencies being planned. Everything and I mean everything was in that file.

Planning didn't stop there, Richard, despite having a full time job and a family, found time to train efficiently and intelligently - it wasn't just about the miles and the hours – it couldn't be. He enlisted my help to work with him on his core, and to help correct muscle imbalances we picked up in his core assessment, as well as Kate Potter from AQR Coaching to work on fitness, skills and (between us) on bike fit.

The dynamic core assessment revealed issues which would have led to injury, either as he ramped up his training or as fatigue set in on the ride, if left unchecked. Working with Kate; Richard's training involved specific exercises to rectify this as well as to develop a strong dynamic core, to help with performance and efficiency. Kate devised a specific training program both to deal with the specific challenges of the Triple as well as to take into account Richard's work and home life commitments.

So on to the support plan. Both Simon and I know 24 hour racing, but 24 hours with a fixed pit is easy. 36 hours with a demanding, moving pit was a completely different challenge. Enlisting support from the other half of AQR's endurance race team, Ant and Rach both being experienced in 24 hour races, meant we could plan to work in 2 overlapping shifts, to make sure we didn't get too tired. I was also particularly conscious of the potential for something to go wrong medically and although I am reasonably well trained, I am no sports doctor. We consulted with numerous experts as to the possible problems we might encounter and did everything we could to minimise risk. The final team was made up of a support van, a camper van, 4 support crew, a Physio (me!), a sports med doctor, and a team of support riders for the last leg – to make sure this crazy idea was as safe as possible.

With all this meticulous planning a date was set – Sunday the 3rd to Monday the 4th June - what could possibly go wrong?

The Weather

A surprise storm coming in after 2 weeks of dry weather meant that the South Downs Way would turn from being perfectly baked to being treacherous, slippery and gloopy. As the forecast firmed up Simon, in charge of logistics, calculated that the best weather window meant pulling the whole thing forward two days – this was on the Thursday morning, which meant we had to go tomorrow. A few phone calls later and it became apparent that a Friday start meant that more than half the team physically could not make it.

15 months of planning thrown up into the air - panic!

I frantically looked through my contacts to see who might be able to stand in. Bingo! Judy and Roy from Dark Star Brewery's endurance team. They were local, also knew the endurance scene and amazingly they were free.

We scrabbled round trying to get more support riders who were free, but with this little notice on an extended bank holiday weekend it was proving a struggle.

Almost sorted and then another phone call from Simon. "We are also changing the route" The normal prevailing wind is from the West, but the storm coming in was bringing in a strong Easterly wind for the final leg, which didn't make sense to ride into on the final leg, so all change to an Eastbourne start rather than Winchester argh!!! By the end of the day my hair was pulled out and lying in a heap on the floor and my biro chewed down to the nib.

37 hours after the start, Richard cruised into Winchester. 15 months after that "innocent question". He had done it; the first person ever to cycle the South Downs Way three times in one shot. The last 37 hours had been utterly brilliant, incredible, scary and exhausting and Richard had been absolutely amazing.

The hours and months of preparation and planning had been worth it. For sure Richard had ridden into the record books, and I don't know many people who could have done that, but the pit crew had been kept busy and not everything had gone to plan. In the end there were seven core members of the support team as well as support riders making sure he was safe. Every single member of that crew contributed and just about every "what if" scenario came into play. I would have hated to have been the one to take the call on whether to stop Richard from continuing when he started to waiver with 60 miles to go. A professional sports medic performing a medical exam and testing for cognitive reasoning confirmed his body was functioning normally despite being exhausted, is just the kind of reassurance we needed; and a fresh set of crew with fresh brains to take on driving duties and question decisions was invaluable towards the end.

So a marker has been set and no doubt someone will try to break it. I know Richard is in many ways an ordinary bloke who has achieved an extraordinary thing, but please don't be tempted into thinking it is easily achievable. If you, like Richard, wake up one day wanting to ride a long, long way without sleep, please grab that thought with both hands and say Yes, but also be aware of the dangers involved. Plan ahead, make your body the best that it can be, get yourself a crew who can look after you, and plan for everything!

Remember, it's about breaking a record, not breaking yourself... Good luck!

Acknowledgements

A massive THANK YOU to everyone who got involved.

The Support Crew

Anne Dickins – for sharing my enthusiasm and for teaching me things I didn't know I needed

Simon Usher – for managing the support crew and keeping the show on the road

Judy McNeill – for being there at every check point looking after the details

Roy McNeil – for popping up all over the place providing extra motivation along the way

Jerry Hill – for the medical assistance to keep me safe, even after my body collapsed

Ant Jordon – for company and subtle guidance during the difficult stages

Rachel Sokal – for travelling a long way to help us and giving the support crew a boost when they needed it most

Support / Safety riders

Dave Brothers - official support rider who changed his weekend plans umpteen times in order to help us

Other riders who just turned up include; Jim Russell, Rory Hitchens, Frazer Clifford, JP Saville, Simon Catmur, John Lemonius, Gavin Thomson, Jo Burt, Lydia Gould and many more

Supporters who came out to see me include; Lydia Gould, Mike Anton, Josh Ibbett, Mark Raffield, the family who live in Petersfield Road Winchester, and probably several others

Mike Anton for capturing the moments with his camera

Josh Ibbett – for donating his prized Torq drink when it was most needed

All the runners and supporters of the South Downs Relay

Advice and Assistance

Fiona, Lorna & Dan for putting up with all my time spent training and for being there at the finish

USE – for providing the Exposure Lights to hide the darkness

My Goodness – for providing the For Goodness Shakes to aid recovery

Kate Potter – for providing the training I needed, which wasn't always the training I wanted

Pete Haines from Kiss Training - for his in depth outdoor first aid advice

Dave Buchanan: Guinness record holder for endurance mountain biking - for his advice on what happens to your body after 24 hours riding

Endomondo followers, Twitter followers and Singletrack World followers and contributors – for tracking my progress and sharing in the enthusiasm for the ride

Singletrack World – permission to reproduce the forum thread and all those who posted comments

Ben Hunt-Davis – for providing the motivation I needed to start cycling and for teaching me how to achieve goals

Book contributors, advisors and helpers

Ben Hunt-Davis, Anne Dickins, Judy McNeill, Simon Catmur, Josh Ibbett, Mike Anton, Fiona Sterry, Tim & Pat Sterry, Louise Poynton, Singletrack World and Twitter followers.

Additional Information

The History of the South Downs Double

With any length of bridleway it's not long before people venture to ride it from end to end. End to end rides are dotted all across the world providing a variety of challenges for the intrepid trail blazer.

Following the 20 mile extension to Winchester in 2005, Ian Butler set out to become the first person to achieve the South Downs Double. It had never been completed before and he wanted to see if it was possible. After 23:01 hours he claimed the title. Since then there has been a slow and steady stream of enthusiasts to reach the exclusive club for sub 24 hour Hall of Fame.

Over a dozen people set out to ride the Double in 2011 where only 5 completed the full length with just 4 making it within 24 hours. Commiserations and congratulations go to Ben Amesbury who got 7 punctures yet carried on to complete his ride. He finally finished in 25:55 hours.

Lydia Gould became the first woman to complete the South Downs Double on 23rd August 2008 in 27:26 hours. The only other female to complete the Double is Grace Henderson on 21st September 2012 in a gruelling 30:51 hours.

Other successful attempts outside 24 hours include Peter Hutson and Roger Easterbrook who happened to ride the Double at the same time I rode my Double in 2009.

Sub 24 hour South Downs Doublers compiled from the South Downs Double web site.

www.southdownsdouble.net

No.	South Downs Double	Date	Time
1st	**Ian Butler** 1st Sub 24 hour Double	September 2005	23:01:00
2nd	**Mike Cotty** New Record	14th June 2006	22:25:22
	Ian Butler	12th August 2007	23:13:00
3rd	**Neil Newell** New Record	29th August 2007	22:20:25
4th	**Rob Lee** New Record 1st unsupported ride	6th May 2008	20:55:51
	Neil Newell 1st Single Speed Unsupported	23rd July 2008	23:20:32
	Mike Cotty New Record Unsupported	26th September 2008	19:52:26
5th	**Ian Leitch** New Record Unsupported	22nd May 2009	18:03:12
6th	**Steve Heading** Steve originally rode a shorter Double in the 1990's. Here he did the full 200 miles.	26th May 2009	20:36:11
7th	**Richard Sterry** 1st Double ride for Charity - BHF	27th June 2009	23:31:00
8th	**Rob Dean**	30th June 2009	19:59:13
9th	**Alan Goldsmith**	2nd August 2009	22:41:45
10th	**Ben Sherratt** Single Speed	25th June 2010	23:40:13

No.	South Downs Double	Date	Time
11th	**Anthony Gray**	25th June 2010	23:05:08
	Rob Dean New Single Speed Record - Unsupported	1st July 2010	18:41:59
12th	**Alan Velecky**	23rd September 2010	23:31:53
13th	**Darren Slade**	12th May 2011	23:38:21
14th	**Paul Gibbons**	15th July 2011	23:36:00
15th	**Kevin Izzard**	19th August 2011	23:19:39
16th	**Josh Ibbett** New Record Unsupported	23rd September 2011	17:47:30
	Richard Sterry 1st two legs of the Triple	1st June 2012	22:55:00
	Richard Sterry 2nd two legs of the Triple	2nd June 2012	26:41:00

Only 4 people had completed the Double when I planned my ride in September 2008. There was very little information available so I spent hours researching the route and studying the reports from those few courageous riders.

It's also interesting to see how many people have ridden the Double more than once, it is strangely addictive. I remember the buzz after finishing my Double in 2009 making me want to do it again. There was no way I could match the tumbling times so I had to find a new way to give it a purposeful meaning.

Advice for a South Downs Double Ride

Racing for 24 hours or participating in an organised event is a breeze compared to riding the South Downs Double or Triple. The event organisers do everything for you, so you just have to turn up and ride your bike. It also helps to do a bit of training beforehand.

Here are some of the additional aspects to think about if you want to take on the South Downs Double. You may want to study this book in detail before thinking about taking on the South Downs Triple.

Unlike an organised event with a set date, you have the wide choice for the time of the year and the day of the week. Naturally the summer is better with the longer days and the generally dryer conditions. Some experienced riders have taken the opportunity of a good weather window, leaving just 2 weeks of final preparation before their Double. If you are attempting the Double for the first time, preparation is the key, try to be flexible with the date in case there is bad weather. I spent 9 months planning my Double ride with the choice of two different weekends. To help with navigation, riding with a full moon will improve night time visibility.

The Double has been achieved from a variety of start locations. Originally Winchester was the favourite with the flatter start and finish, and then riders chose Eastbourne to coincide with the BHF Randonnee event, whilst some have started from the middle. Personally I think it sounds better going from one end to the other.

Once a date and start location is chosen, think carefully about the start time. Consider your natural body clock and the duration of darkness. Setting out first thing in the morning will leave the night riding till the end when you are tired. Alternatively, starting in the evening will help with the night riding but tiredness can set in on the second leg. Looking up the sunrise and sunset times will help calculate the number of hours of darkness. If you're going for a record attempt you can almost avoid any night riding. Experienced mountain bike racer Ian Leitch chose well by starting at 3am and finished at 9pm. He was just in time for a pint at the pub in Winchester.

The www.southdownsdouble.net_web site has the official South Downs Double route. Check the directions carefully as there are some variations with the route currently marked and that used by the BHF. Over the years the National Trust has altered their route making the choice of which one to use more difficult.

Some prefer to ride the traditional (pre 2009) route of the South Downs Way to perhaps compare times with earlier rides, or because it is slightly shorter. Others take on the official South Downs Way route with the 2009 variation near Exon and the 2012 extension at Eastbourne. Either way both options count as the South Downs Way, but if you are going for a record ride you will need to choose carefully which one you do.

So many people have got lost on the South Downs where they have missed a turning and descended into the wrong valley. I remember years ago taking the wrong fork near Devils Dyke and being faced with a 300 foot climb to get back onto the ridge. It cost us an extra 20 minutes along with a large amount of physical and mental energy.

The South Downs Way signs with the blue acorns mark out the route but sometimes you need to be observant to spot them. Some signs and turnings are not immediately obvious, which can easily be overshot especially at speed. Study the maps very carefully noting any turnings or forks. It is also easy to miss some turnings when travelling in the opposite direction.

In several locations the South Downs Way bridleway runs alongside a road. For an official Double, the bridleways must be used. I know it easier on the road but the nature of the challenge is to ride the South Downs Way and not the South Downs Road.

At night time it is much easier to follow well defined tracks whereas crossing open fields is more difficult in the dark. The killer is thick fog, which often occurs in the summer as well as winter. Visibility can be reduced to just a few feet on high ground making navigation extremely difficult. This is where it is handy to have a GPS even if you think you know the route. Going up Butser Hill near QECP on my Double ride the visibility was only 10-15 feet. Ascending up the steepest part and keeping on the shortest grass got me to the fence half way up, but I missed the gate by about 50 feet.

The most challenging part of the ride are the relentless hills. They are in abundance at the Eastbourne end with the hardest section being from Eastbourne to Ditchling Beacon. The hills appear to go on forever with steep descents. It is often easier, yet slower, to walk up the steepest hills. Make the most of this opportunity off the bike to grab something to eat and use different muscles.

After conquering the hills, the South Downs Way throws out another challenge in the form of gates. There are 190-200 gates encountered during a Double ride, requiring a lot of stopping and starting. Learning how to open gates without unclipping your feet will save a bit of time and effort. If you get really bored or need motivation, you can count them.

Whilst it is reassuring to have riders accompany you on the Double, unless otherwise stated, it is meant to be a solo effort. If other riders are with you, you will need to set the pace and open the gates as if you are riding solo.

This may be a 24 hour event for you and if you have a support crew it will also be a 24 hour event for them. Unlike normal 24 hour racing around a circuit, the support crew will need to navigate to the next meeting place. Build in some rest times for the crew with a longer distance between some check points. I gave my crew on the Double a 2 hour rest between Winchester and the QECP when they could grab 40 winks. Supply loads of food and refreshments for your crew. I even provided some in car entertainment for them in the form of the Blackadder Goes Forth

CD – apparently this helped them to keep awake in the early hours.

As you can choose your places to meet up with the support crew, space them out so they can reach the location in time. It can take a while to follow the South Downs Way on the roads, sometimes it is quicker to ride trail that is more direct. If possible select Check Point locations to be at the top of hills. They will motivate you on the way up the hill and you won't have a dreaded climb immediately after a break. If you are going to ride a part of the Double with the BHF event, some of their check points have limited parking facilities.

Do have a plan in place if the support crew are not at the expected Check Point, with at least two means of communication between yourself and the crew. You never know what might happen to either of you.

If you are riding unsupported make a note of the public water taps along the South Downs Way. It is worth having a backup plan in case the tap you want is not working.

A GPS is good for navigation and to validate your ride, but the battery may fail before you do. I made an external battery pack for my Garmin Edge 705 whereas some riders have used a fresh GPS for the return leg.

To qualify for the South Downs Double, your ride will need to be verified. Check for what is acceptable evidence with the adjudicators on the www.southdownsdouble.net site. A GPS log or photographs with a timing clock at specific locations could be used.

Completing the South Downs Double is a fantastic challenge, which has only been accomplished by a few. Be aware that it's a tough cookie. Whether you are a regular long distance rider or just a weekend warrior, it's a mighty achievement that will keep you smiling for a long time.

About the Author

No one is going to do it for you unless you do it yourself, was one of the lessons I learned at boarding school near Maidstone. Seeking independence I had my bike at school which enabled me to cycle the 50 miles home on the occasional weekend when we were allowed out. No one showed me which way to go; I planned my own route and just got on with it.

Setting out in a career of Electronics, I then found my niche in IT. As a new manager I felt others had something that I was lacking but I couldn't put my finger on it. Ben's training course on the Power of Belief hit the nail right on the head and set me off in a new direction of personal development.

Taking up cycling again aged 36 I refined the art of goal setting to accomplish more and more. Riding on the North Downs I would regularly gravitate towards Brockets Farm for a cuppa and a piece of their special Tiffin cake.

I met Fiona at my local church in Reigate, Surrey, we married in 1989 and our twins Lorna and Dan were born in 1995. They have successfully made it through the compulsory education years where they now have solid foundations to choose whatever they want for their lives.

Encouraging and motivating others gives me great pleasure especially when I can see the improvements later in their lives. It would be an honour for me to help someone to achieve a really crazy goal.

Richard Sterry

Lightning Source UK Ltd.
Milton Keynes UK
UKOW03f1859050813

214918UK00020B/1479/P